Watercolor *Fun and*

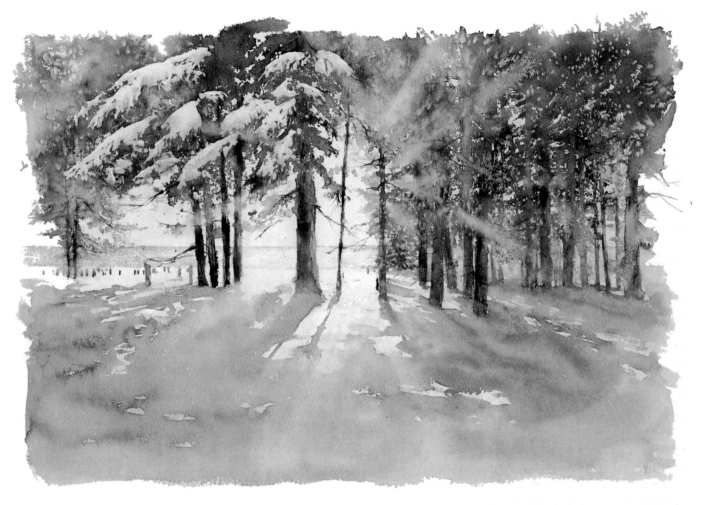

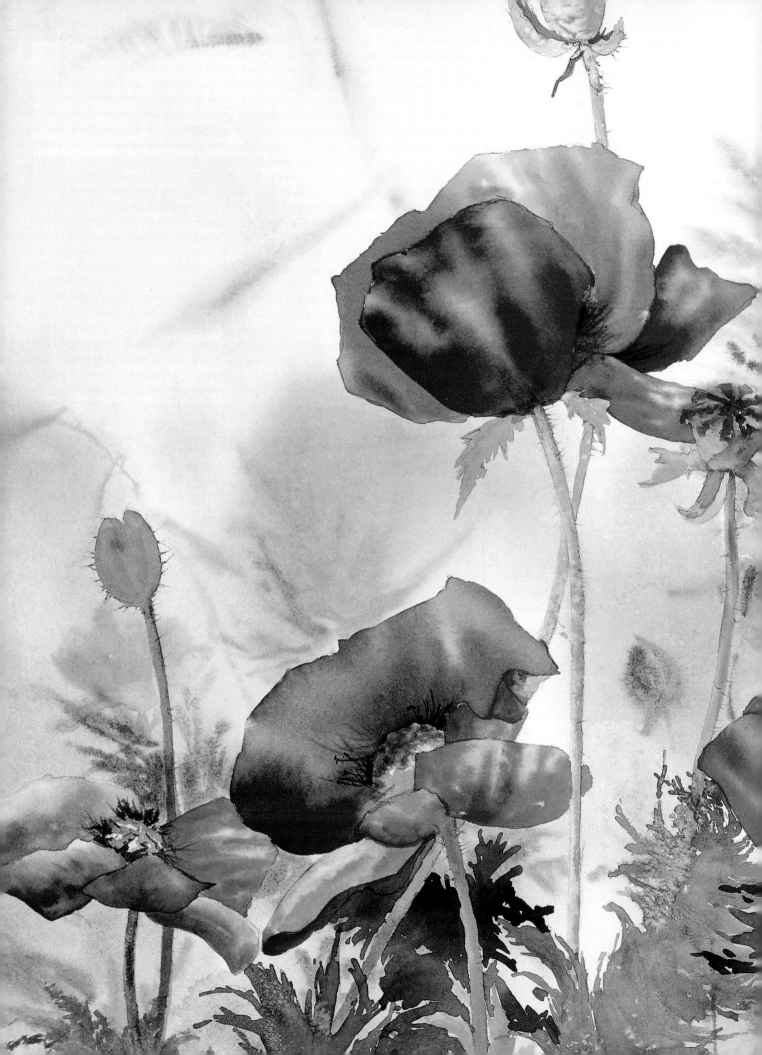

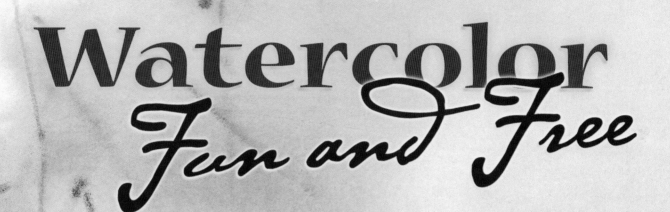

Watercolor
Fun and Free

Karlyn Holman

Bayfield Street Publishing, Inc.
Washburn, Wisconsin

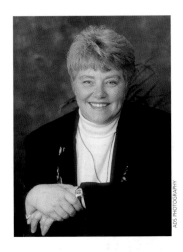

Karlyn Holman has had a studio/gallery since 1968 and enjoys being a full-time painter, gallery owner and workshop teacher. Karlyn has always lived by the shores of Lake Superior and has derived inspiration for her watercolor paintings from the beauty of that area, as well as from her travels around the world. Her paintings have been described as realism based on abstract structure, yet they remain experimental in nature. She has illustrated four children's picture books and one illustrated book. She has taught on location in England, Italy, Norway, Sweden, Russia, Guatemala, Greece, France, Portugal, the Yucatan, China, Hong Kong, Bangkok, Singapore, Ireland, Bulgaria, and on three cruises in the Caribbean. Karlyn always knew she wanted to be an artist and pursued this dream through college, receiving an MA in Art from the University of Wisconsin. She taught art at the college level for ten years and currently teaches high-energy watercolor workshops around the world. Karlyn's enthusiastic and humorous teaching style makes beginners feel comfortable yet challenges advanced students.

Karlyn and her husband, Gary, have three adult children and six grandchildren, and are both natives of Washburn, Wisconsin, a small village on the south shore of Lake Superior. Visit her on the web at www.karlynholman.com.

Bayfield Street Publishing, Inc.
116-1/2 East 5th Street
Washburn, Wisconsin 54891
(715) 373-1040
baypub@cheqnet.net

10 9 8 7 6 5 4 3 2 1
Edited by Teresa Wagner and Jan Esposito
Designed by Jan Esposito, Printing Plus/Screen Line
Photography by Karlyn Holman, unless otherwise noted

Printed in China by Everbest Printing Company through
Four Colour Imports, Louisville, Kentucky

Library of Congress Cataloging-in-Publication Data

Holman, Karlyn.
    Watercolor Fun and Free / Karlyn Holman; [edited by] Teresa J. Wagner.–1.
    p. ; cm.
    ISBN 0-9670683-2-0 (alk. paper) -- ISBN 0-9670683-3-9 (pbk.)
    L Wagner, Teresa J. II. Title.

00-102855

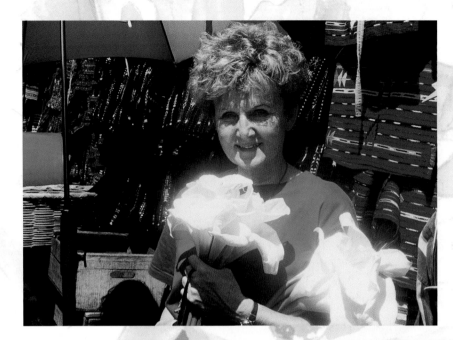

Dedicated to the memory of Joan Simpson,
a talented artist and dear friend.

I would like to thank the following people:

Bonnie Broitzman, Adell Bruns, the contributing
artists and my many artist and mentor friends, for
sharing their wealth of knowledge, their love of
watercolor, their friendship and their affinity for
having fun.

John Teeter, my publisher, for his confidence
and expertise.

Teresa Wagner, my editor, for her gift for crafting
words, wise counsel and friendship.

Jan Esposito, for polishing my rough copy and fine
tuning my vision into a beautiful presentation.

Rose Edin, an outstanding watercolor artist, for
inviting me to co-host international painting tours
with her. This experience has been invaluable to
my growth as an artist.

Stan Edin, for sharing his expertise on
photography.

Mary Rice, for inspiring me to make traveling
an adventure.

My husband, Gary, my children and grandchildren,
my mom and the memory of my father, for their
love and support.

Table of Contents

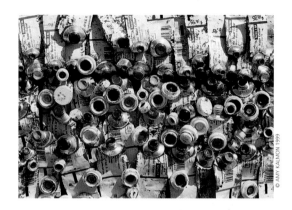

© AMY KALMON 1999

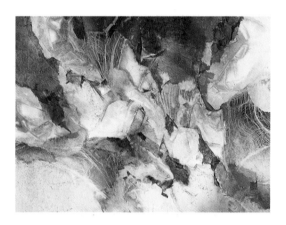

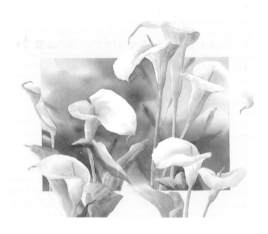

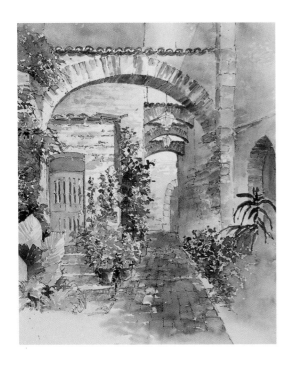

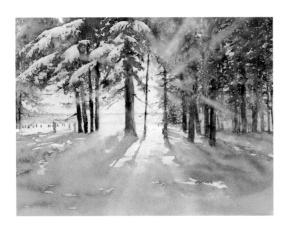

Introduction

My lifelong passion has been to be an artist. When I was a child, my parents not only gave me unconditional love, they also made sure I had a great selection of art supplies and encouragement to feed my soul. My journey as an artist had begun.

There is no one medium or form of expression that is better than another. The important elements are *passion* and *personal vision*. My passion is watercolor! In the late '70s, I was busy painting in oils, making pottery and running a studio/gallery. I was also a wife, raising three children, seven foster children, and teaching college part time. Susan Stringe, a local artist, introduced me to watercolor and it was love at first sight. While I continued to work in all my other media, I began to focus more and more on watermedia. I loved the discovering, the experimenting, the transparency, and most of all, the spontaneity of watercolor, which allowed me to paint even if only for short periods of time. Now, every time I pick up a color and charge it into a wet wash, I fall in love all over again.

This book presents a wide variety of approaches, both traditional and non-objective, and each demonstration offers a unique way to express your subject matter. Sometimes, switching approaches is a good way to stay inspired and to keep the experience on a *fun and free* level. These demonstrations are not intended to be "formulas" to follow, but merely techniques and ideas to try on your own personal journey through the world of watercolor. The joy you experience and the sense of well-being you feel when you paint are the ultimate gifts of watercolor—a return to the child within us all.

My passion for watercolor evolved into teaching watermedia workshops. I have often been told, "Don't share all your secrets!" The real truth is, I have no secrets. Sharing and exchanging ideas has been the most rewarding part about being a teacher, because I learned to understand and distill technical information into concepts that students can easily grasp. My goal has always been to teach technical information, share ideas, and hope the students will discover their own paths. Teaching has challenged me to constantly evaluate what is important in the students' journey towards self-realization, and I often use humor to help them overcome fear or discouragement along the way. I feel great joy when I see an experienced artist helping a beginner. This bonding and sharing and encouraging is what workshops and retreats are all about.

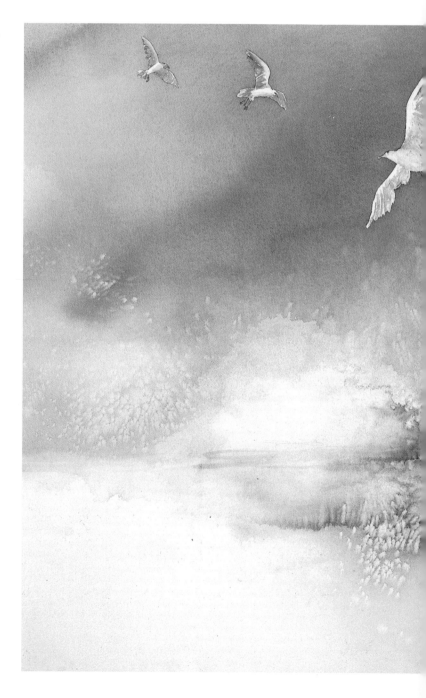

This book uses the same format that I use in my workshops and is organized around three subject areas: abstraction, flowers, and landscapes. Each of the seventeen demonstrations specifies a particular technique, ranging from traditional layered washes to a more "alla prima" (all at once) approach. Not all paintings are successes, so at the end of several chapters, I offer some techniques for saving those "less than perfect" paintings. Taking risks exposes you to the possibility of producing unsuccessful paintings; however, each painting that does not meet your expectations brings you a step closer to understanding the expansive nature of watercolor. The more you pursue watercolor, the more you will discover and the more excited you will become. The transparency and immediacy of watercolor are addicting! Stay enthused, keep working, and make every painting the best it can be. Maintain an adventurous attitude, build a foundation for finding your own personal expression, and keep the experience *fun and free.*

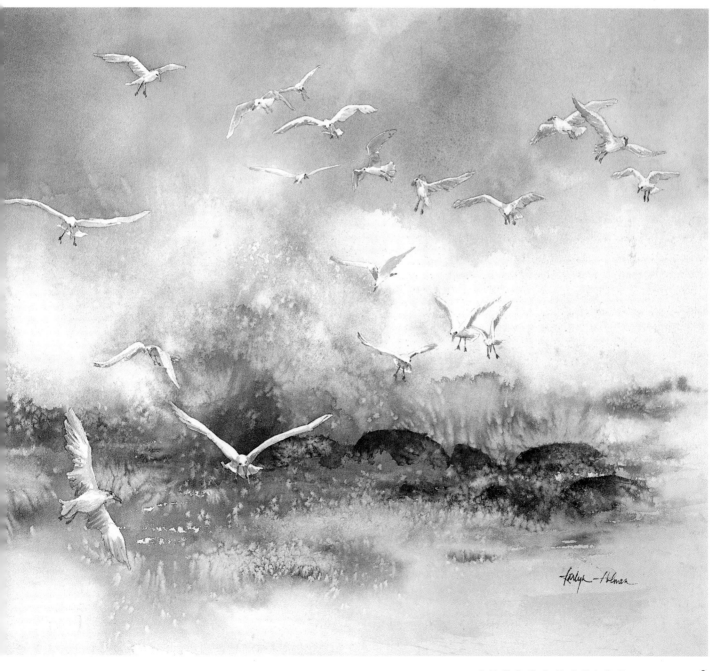

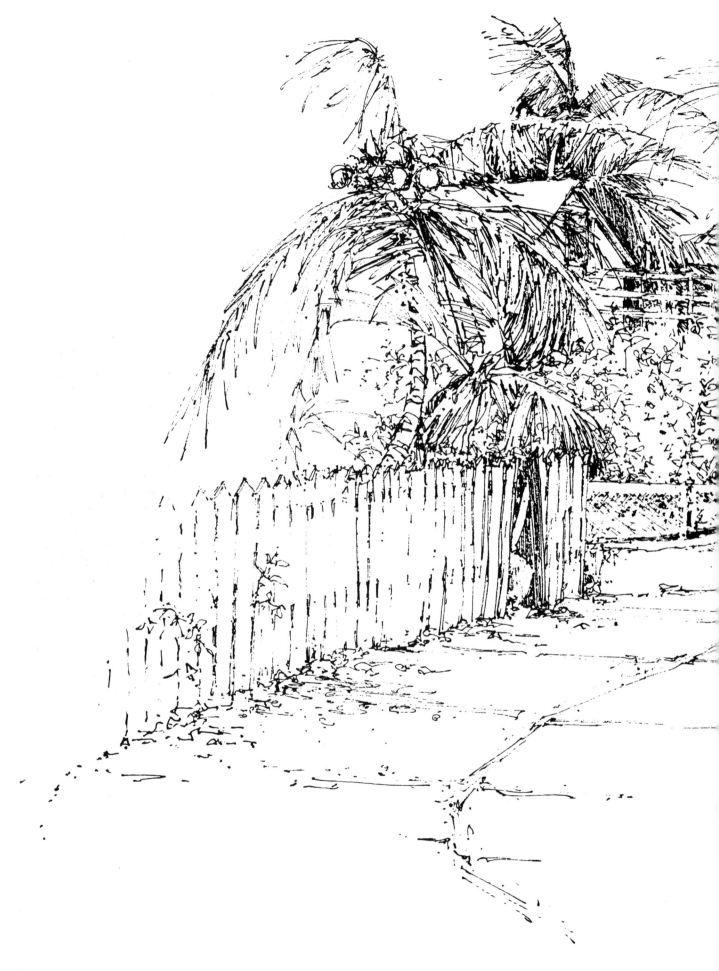

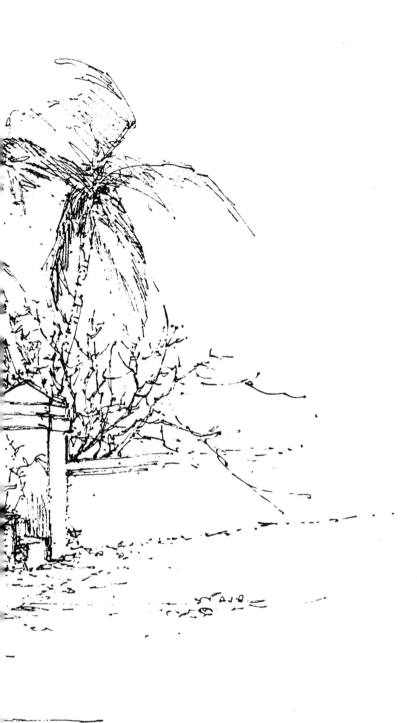

CHAPTER ONE
Searching for inspiration

What inspires you to paint? Most inspiration comes from what we experience and know. I always ask my friends and students what inspires them to paint and the responses always amaze me...the tranquility of a medieval village, the changing light on a building, the view out a window, the smile on a child's face, the painting process itself, the desire to express emotions, a workshop with friends, changing seasons, journal writing. Your inspiration is your own personal muse.

To begin in watercolor, you must make choices about your personal selection of colors, brushes, and paper, but the most important tool is your own *mind's eye*. How can you take your thoughts, feelings, and perceptions and translate them to paper?

Watercolor is both a reflection of the subject and the artist. Everything you perceive is interpreted by your heart and eventually reflected in the finished painting. All art is very personal—each time you paint a picture, you paint something about yourself. The way you apply your brushstrokes, the colors you use, and especially the subjects you choose to paint all show your individuality. The essence of watercolor lies in the excitement of creation and the fulfillment you feel when you finish a painting.

Exploring materials that work for you

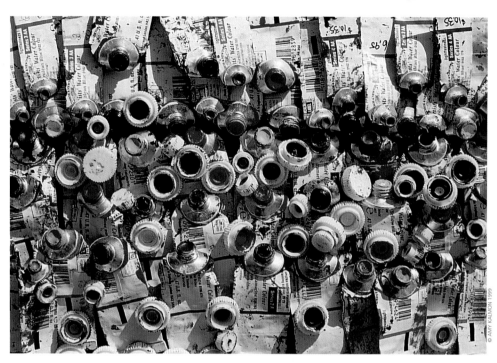

As artists, we are always looking for that happy brush or magic tool that will transform our paintings into masterpieces. This process of choice involves research and trial and error. Just when you think you have found the perfect colors, along come the man-made, truly transparent colors like quinacridone burnt orange and ultramarine turquoise and the fun starts all over again.

Studio. The world can be your studio if you travel, but when you are home, having your own studio space is critical. You need to set up everything in a convenient, organized way that works for you. If you have to set up and take down everything every time you paint, the joy and excitement of painting can get lost in the drudgery of process. I will paint even if I only have five minutes. My first "studio" was a table in a corner of my dining room. I had three children under the age of three, so I organized space for them and we all painted together. Once my studio was set up, I never took it down, even during formal dinner parties. I often hear artists say, "When my kids leave, I am going to set up a studio space." Why wait—do it now! Choose a spot with good light, full of inspiration and comfort, and claim it as your own.

After my dining room days, I graduated to a closet-sized space in my dusty pottery studio, which I shared with four other potters. I decided to move to the attic to get away from the dust. My husband saved the day by expanding the attic into a second story. While he pounded nails, I planned how to use every square inch of that space. When you design your own studio, plan for a lot of storage space, an area to do your bookkeeping and letter writing, an area to photograph your

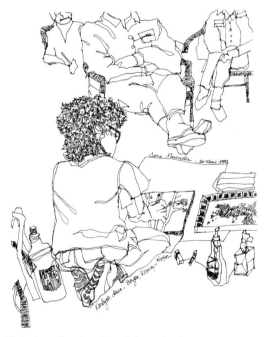

This drawing by Sara Muender is a contour drawing of me "in my studio" demonstrating while traveling on a ferry boat in Norway, 1992. Notice how she uses a continuous line.

work, and most importantly, a properly-lit painting area. Check out full spectrum lighting, which mimics daylight and is extremely important for color accuracy. Remember that a studio can be a corner of your dining room as long as it is *your space*.

I have listed my current choices of materials, but this list is always subject to change.

Palettes. I use two palettes: a small compact one for travel and my round palette for teaching and for painting in my studio. The simplest and most significant choice I have made is to set up my paints like a color wheel. By doing so, I place the colors in their harmonic and complementary positions. If you do the research and then put the colors in their proper position on the wheel, you will have a constant reminder of their physical properties. The colors are either a warm red or cool red, warm blue or cool blue, etc. This visual reminder will help you learn to make more effective color choices.

Colors. Color choices are very personal and your preferences may change. Because there are more color choices than ever before, you should carefully research what is available and then make your decision. My personal choice is to limit my palette to a variety of primaries with a few secondary colors. The most powerful tool an artist has is his or her color identity. I can often determine who painted a picture because I recognize the artist's palette long before I look at the signature on the painting.

I used to work in earthy, subdued colors, but now have the confidence to use a brighter palette. My current palette consists of mostly warm and cool versions of primary colors, and I try not to clutter my selections with premixed greens or browns. By working predominantly with transparent primary colors, my paintings will stay relatively mud-free. When you work with premixed greens or browns, you have no idea what colors were used to make them. Try mixing your own greens, and then try some of the quinacridone colors and add vitality to your paintings.

Fill your paint wells to the top with color and let them dry. Then, whenever you start painting, the colors are easily activated. Transparency (allowing the white of the paper to show through the colors), tinting strength (power to influence other colors in a mixture), and intensity (purity and brightness) are all part of the process of getting to know your paint choices. Always choose "artist" quality rather than "student" quality paints. Once you have determined your color choices, memorize their position on the palette and you will always know what color you are using.

Color wheel labels:
aureolin yellow
Winsor yellow
Winsor green (blue shade)
raw sienna
ultramarine turquoise
Winsor orange
antwerp blue
scarlet lake
cerulean blue
quinacridone burnt orange
indigo
Winsor red
cobalt blue
permanent alizarin crimson
ultramarine blue
permanent rose
permanent magenta

Paper. Paper choice is important, because the texture, absorbency and whiteness differ from paper to paper. I select paper that is 100% acid-free. For each demonstration in the book, I will indicate the paper I am using. I seldom stretch my paper because it never ends up flat anyway. Applying paint on the paper surface can create uneven drying, which will buckle even stretched paper. I wait until I have a frameable piece and flatten it by saturating the back of the painting with water and laying it between two layers of blotter paper with a substantial weight on top. Using this method, I can flatten as many paintings as I have ready to frame. I let them stay under the weight until they are dry. The drying time will vary, depending on the humidity in the air. I now have a heat press and can flatten anything in ten minutes, so I never bother to stretch anything anymore.

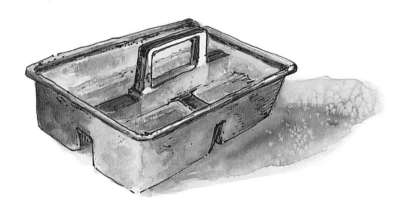

Water bucket. I like to use a shallow container, so I can touch the bottom with the brush in order to release the paint. I love my "three-holer" because it provides three sources of clean water. When you use a shallow container, you also avoid getting water into the ferrule of the brush which may accidentally drip onto your painting.

Brushes. Brushes are another personal choice. I prefer synthetic brushes because they have body and can take abuse. Sable brushes are much softer and are wonderful for layering color over a surface that is prone to lifting.

I use six styles of brushes, each with a specific purpose:

Wash brush. I use a 1-1/2" wash brush for wetting the paper. In fact, I paint just about all my abstract paintings with this brush because it really holds a lot of paint and moves it around with great accuracy.

Round. I have several sizes of rounds, which I mostly use for my floral and landscape paintings. Small rounds are great for detail and larger rounds are perfect for laying in color. The bristles of a round brush are tapered to a point and provide variety in your brushstrokes.

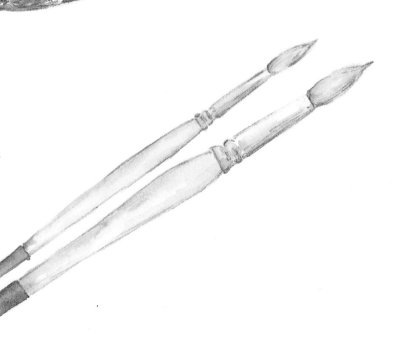

Flat. I use 1/4" and 1/2" flat brushes for two reasons. Using a flat brush allows you to paint a nice, crisp line. This brush is also the best brush for lifting color because all the bristles are the same length. I always use one of these brushes when lifting the white shapes in reflections.

Script. This long-haired brush is great for details such as rigging on a boat or grasses. I also use it to apply masking because the smaller number of bristles makes cleaning the mask out of the brush easier. I wet the brush, saturate it with soap, dip the brush in the masking, and then apply the masking to the paper.

Oriental. This brush is made from natural hair; therefore, it releases the paint easily, unlike synthetic brushes which hold the paint. I use this releasing technique to make patterns of water which later become patterns of foliage. Then, using the same brush, I can easily throw paint into these puddles of water.

Scrubber. This is an oil painter's brush cut down to half its size, so it is very stiff. I wet the brush, and by applying a firm motion, I can lift the color off the paper. A scrubber can be very destructive to the paper, so I only use it on final details.

These materials are used on occasion for various projects throughout the book. Arranged from left to right: webbing spray, metallic spray, mister and sprayer, masking, gauze, matte medium and varnish, glue and brayer.

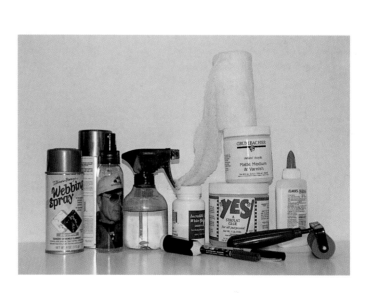

Drawing...finding the line between your heart and your hand

Drawing gives you the confidence to tackle any subject. If you first draw the image you want to paint, that drawing becomes the bones of the painting itself. I have had a lifelong infatuation with drawing, which is, after all, nothing more than taking your observations and your feelings and recording them on paper. Learning to observe the world and to draw what you see is how you grow as an artist.

Drawing is often thought of as something separate from painting, but you can draw with a brush, just as you can paint with water-soluble pencils and water-based pens. Painting is an extension of drawing. The two are so closely related that if you nurture the relationship between them, your work will be greatly enhanced.

When you draw, your special marks on the paper come from your heart, not your drawing tools. You make the image, not your pencil. Take all the time you need to practice "seeing" with your heart—a little time every day will be the best investment you can make for yourself.

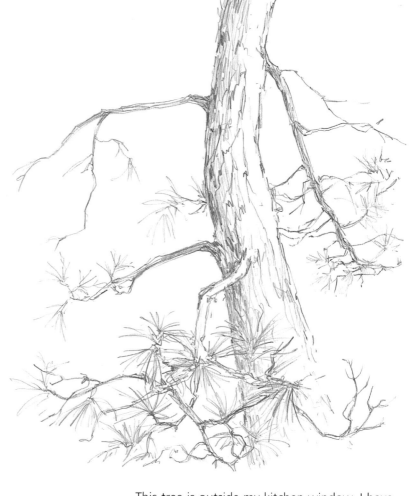

This tree is outside my kitchen window. I have painted and drawn it in all seasons.

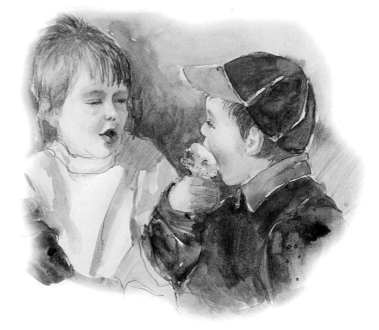

I would rather work with live models, but children do not stop moving long enough to study them. A photo served as inspiration for this sketch of my grandchildren, Tyler and Jordan.

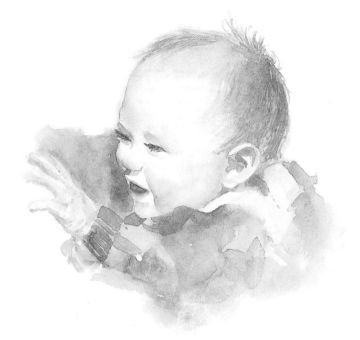

Find the tool that inspires you

Many artists prefer to do their preliminary drawing with a **brush** loaded with paint. This approach is truly "alla prima!" A line drawn with paint on a brush has more variety than a continuous line made by a pencil or a pen. The brush can give a wet or a dry look.

This sketch of my grandson, Brodie, was drawn with paint, using only cobalt blue and permanent magenta.

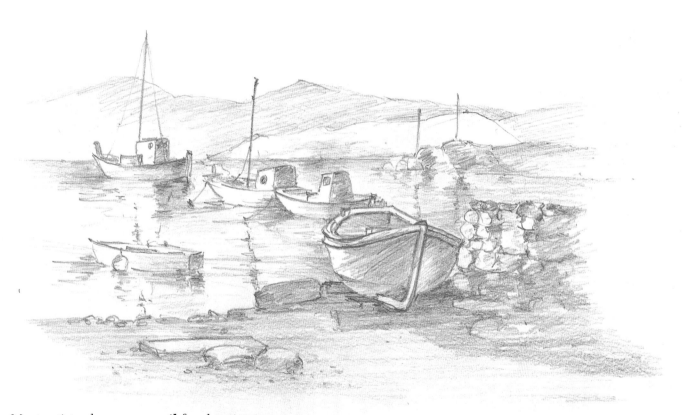

Most artists choose a **pencil** for drawing because the lines can be erased. Having the flexibility to change lines and plan the painting allows you more freedom of interpretation when you actually begin to paint. Pencils come in a range from hard (H) to soft (B). The hard lead is not dark enough to produce a visible line and can engrave the paper. The soft lead, in the high range of 4B to 6B, can leave graphite smudges. I usually use a HB, not too hard and not too soft.

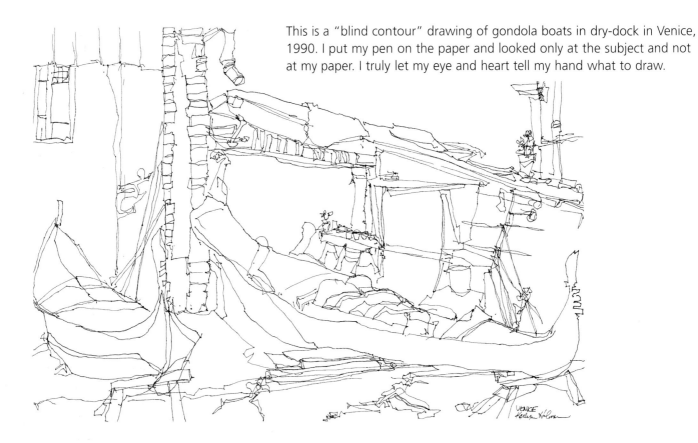

This is a "blind contour" drawing of gondola boats in dry-dock in Venice, 1990. I put my pen on the paper and looked only at the subject and not at my paper. I truly let my eye and heart tell my hand what to draw.

Many artists prefer to draw with **permanent ink** because these lines cannot be erased. The next time you interpret an on-location subject, try using a permanent pen. This "alla prima" style of drawing is daring and moves you more quickly into the actual painting process. With practice, you will find that you can interpret your subject with lively, vital pen lines and still have time to paint before departure. My choice is the "throwaway" pen. I used to carry ink and refill my pen, but it was too risky. After one incident of spilled ink and hours of helping students unclog pens, I moved on to the "throwaways."

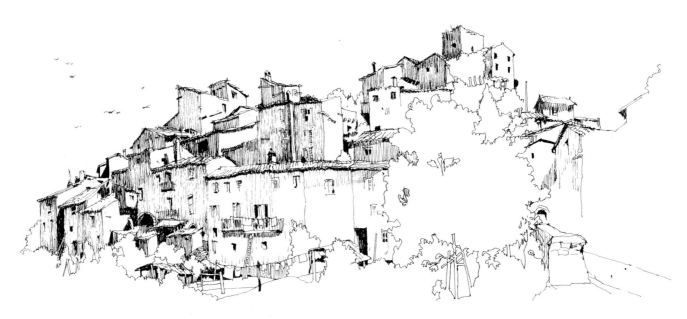

Betty Lynch, well-known watercolorist and sketch artist, drew this medieval hill town of Valle Di San Martino, Italy. Her drawings have a vitality and liveliness derived from working on location. Betty translates life into line. She draws everywhere she goes, rain or shine. "Sketching," says Betty, "is a way to realize and refine what you already know instinctively."

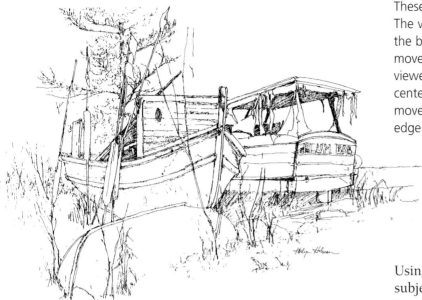

These boats in dry-dock make a great subject. The wooden planks help me understand how the boat was built and add interesting lines of movement. The overturned canoe leads the viewer into the painting. The boats provide the center of interest, and the tree creates vertical movement that reaches out to touch the top edge of the paper.

Using a pen really makes you *look* at your subject. As your drawing develops, you will inevitably make inaccurate marks, but by using your creative energy and adding more lines, you eventually will find the right ones. Making alterations can be challenging and forces you to be inventive. You can cheat a little by using a pencil to draw the directional lines of movement and big shapes. After allowing yourself a few pencil lines for inspiration, get out your pen and experience the excitement of drawing directly on the paper. When you simply copy over pencil lines with a pen, you forfeit the energy of an "alla prima" pen drawing. Using a pen makes you really look at your subject and draw with your heart.

MARY DRIVES TO STOCKHOLM and NAP TIME FOR MARY were drawn by Sara Muender. She has a whimsical style that is very entertaining and it works beautifully with the permanent pen lines. Sara finds inspiration to draw everywhere she travels.

Drawing is the key to painting any subject

If I can draw it, I can paint it. For a long time I was timid about painting figures and portraits. I would draw them but never attempt to paint them. Now I realize that drawing and painting are really an extension of one another, and as I draw a subject, I cannot wait to paint it. Why not challenge yourself to paint a subject you have never painted before?

When I visit museums, I enjoy the drawings as much as the paintings. Artists speak to us through their drawings, because the lines they use to interpret the image reveal their thought processes.

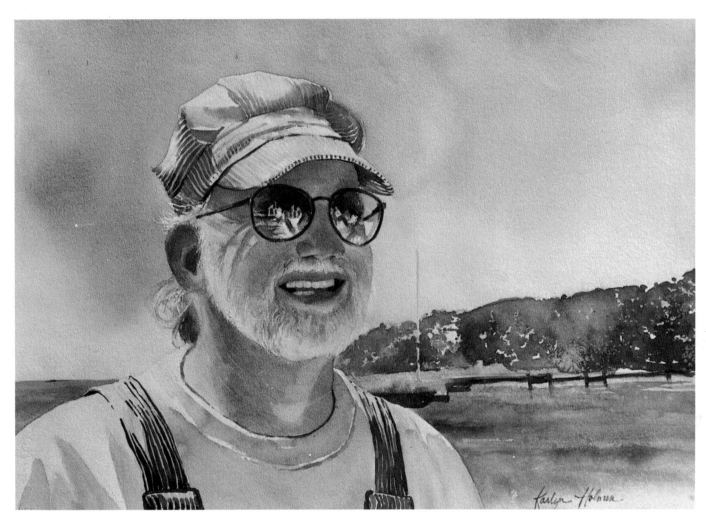

The reflections of the houses in Steve's glasses and the unlikely railroad hat were the inspiration for this painting.

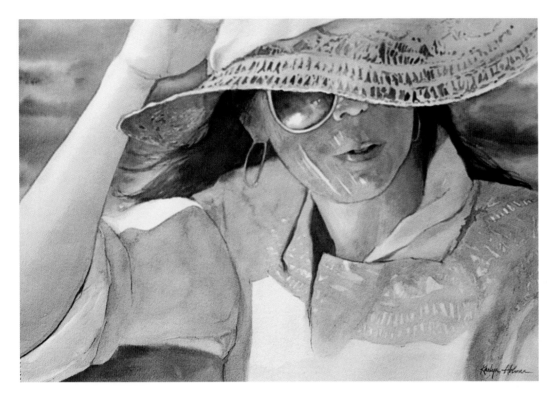

The cast shadows from Susan's hat added visual excitement to this subject.

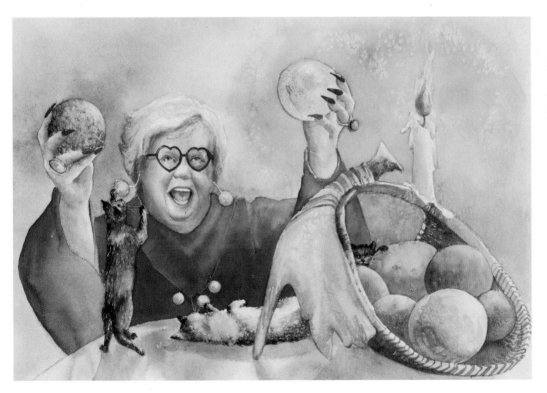

This oldest, coldest witch is calling down the high winds to stir up trouble. This illustration is in *Ditch of Witches*, Bayfield Street Publishing, 1999, a children's picture book written by Warren Nelson.

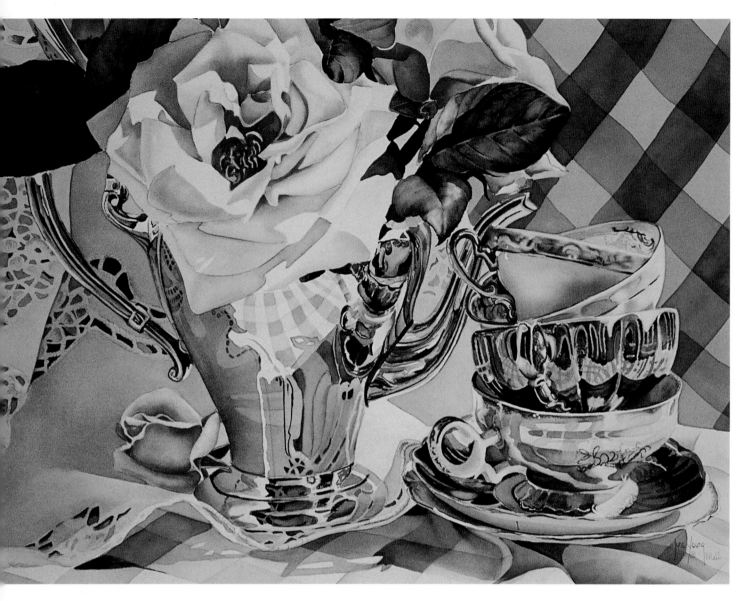

ROSES AND TEACUPS by June Young. About six years ago, June felt frustrated because her paintings were not improving at the rate that she thought they should. "I knew the reason was because I was unable to paint what I saw; I was painting what I thought I saw. My solution was to paint something I had never painted before, something that would make me pay attention to the little things, because I knew if I could do that, the whole painting would take care of itself. Painting still lifes was the answer. I chose various smooth and textured objects and observed the way light fractured and reflected off these objects, and found that the changing play of light is often the key element of the painting. My mother gave me one of her teacups and saucers, which started a small collection for me that I have used many times in my paintings. In this painting, the teapot was an auction find and the roses were a gift. I now pay far greater attention to details. I see color in objects better and I have a greater understanding of the importance of hard and soft edges and where to use them. I have learned to use light to add drama to all the subjects that I paint."

I spent a long time on the drawing for MARY'S PORCH CHAIRS, due to the intricacy of the subject. The time was well spent because the drawing provided a great blueprint for the resulting painting. The actual time spent painting was minimal.

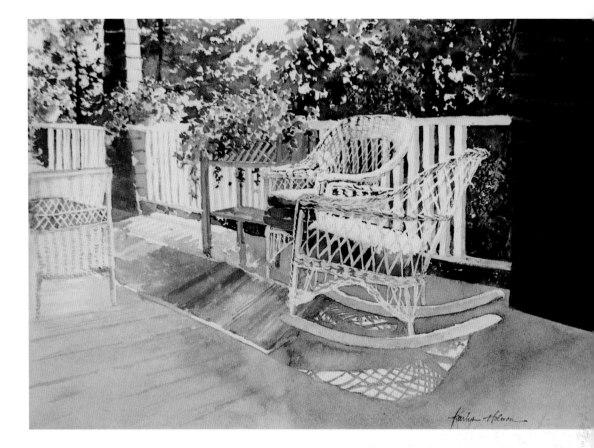

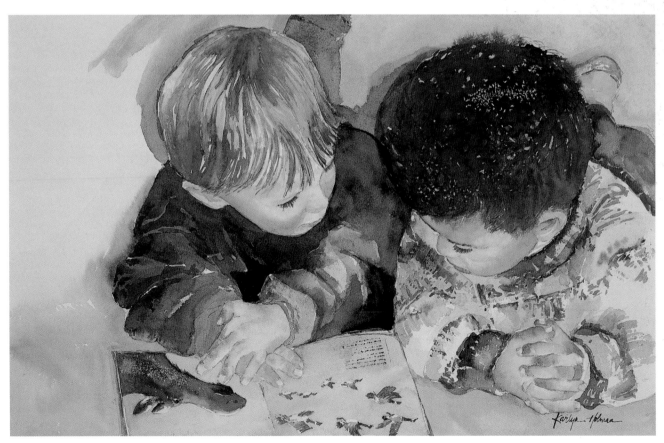

Tyler and Clinton reading *Little Brother Moose* by James Kasperson, Dawn Publications, 1995. This work is another example of a painting that I could not have painted without having spent a lot of time really observing my subject. The key to painting is to practice "seeing" and drawing the subjects you want to paint. As in any other discipline, practice is the key word.

Using the camera as an inspirational tool

The camera can record light, action, people, places and capture images for later interpretation. Many artists do not like to admit that they paint from photographs, while others deny they even use them. Some artists copy them exactly. The important thing to keep in mind is the painting itself…as an artist, how you produce a finished painting is up to you to decide. I have tried to paint market scenes, birds, waves and many subjects that are constantly moving and found it to be an exercise in frustration. I have had a hard time compromising my need to be realistic and accurate by merely reducing the subject to a symbol. Freezing the subject in a photograph allows me time to study and interpret the subject more accurately.

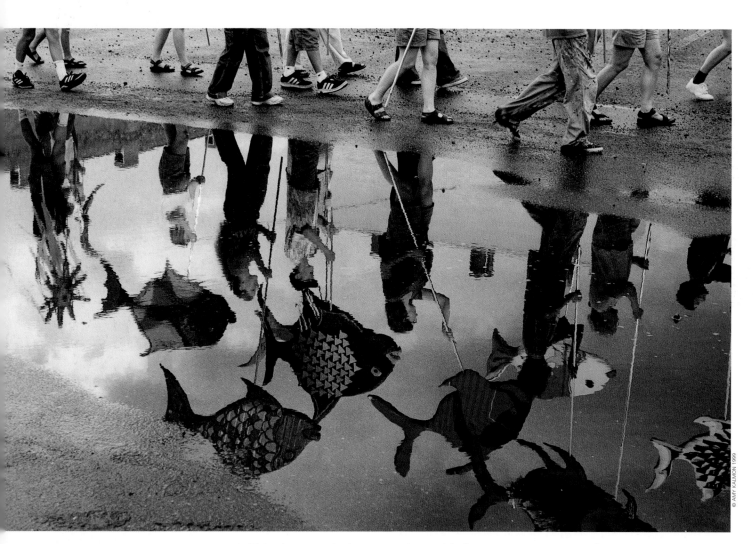

This photograph, by Amy Kalmon titled Rehearse the Revelry, of "St. Esprit Revelry," an art parade by David Genzler and volunteers, shows people reflecting in a puddle of water and captures a moment in time. The only way to study and interpret a subject like this is to freeze the image on film.

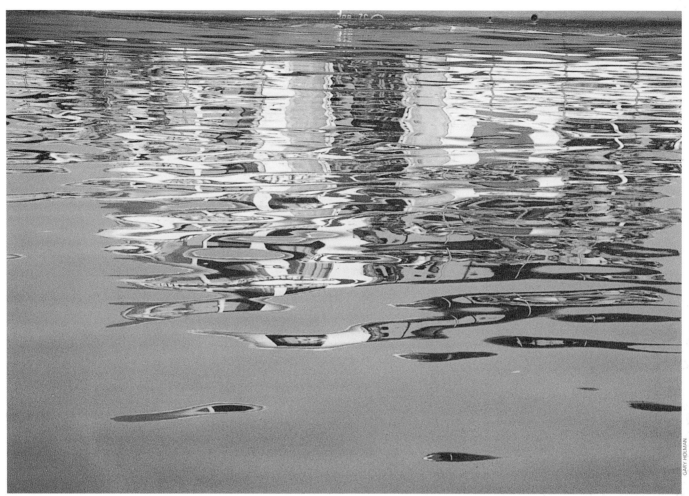

The reflections of a passing boat in Suzhou, China, resulted in these broken shapes in the water. A photo like this could be an inspiration for an abstract interpretation.

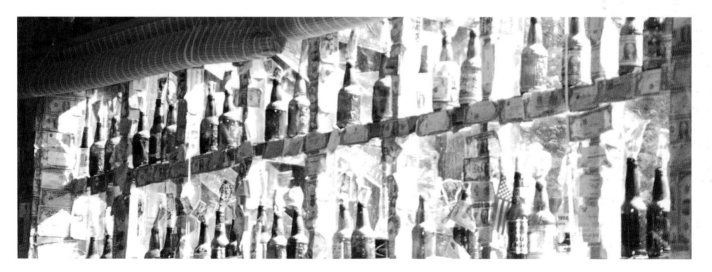

The fractured lighting coming through the window and reflecting on these bottles in a bar in Arizona provides a possible future reference. The subject itself may not be appealing, but the light patterns are certainly unique. A spur-of-the-moment snapshot like this could inspire many paintings that have no resemblance to the original photo.

Using your camera on location

After many years of painting on location, I have found my camera is an invaluable tool. The point-and-shoot camera is especially great because it is lightweight and easy to carry. After I have chosen a painting site, I use my camera as a *viewfinder*. As I am searching for a subject for my painting, I take the time to evaluate both vertical and horizontal formats. I also decide whether the subject should be interpreted close up or using a panoramic view. The camera frames in the subject and helps me make these decisions.

When you look through the viewfinder of a point-and-shoot camera, it is very obvious where the horizon line or eye level falls. The camera distorts your perspective just enough so you can see the exaggerated direction of the lines of movement.

If you have a SLR (single lens reflex) camera, a reliable method is to blur the image in and out of focus to help simplify the subject. If you take the camera all the way out of focus, you will simplify the image into a pattern of abstract shapes and colors.

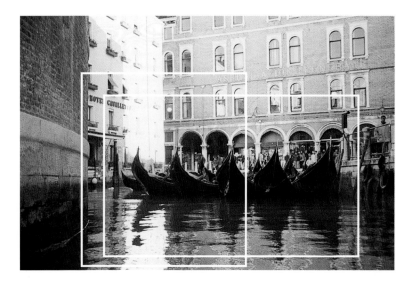

Many photos, such as this photo taken in Venice, have dynamic horizontal and vertical contrasts, but may lack the inspiration to motivate you to start painting. Consider cropping the photo to a more myopic viewpoint. If you edit the extraneous and boring information and concentrate on the parts you like, you will be more inspired to start painting.

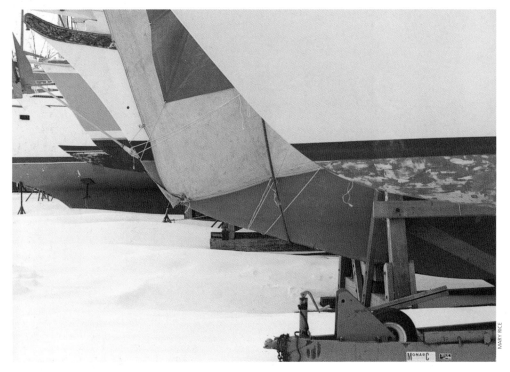

By moving in close with her camera, Mary turned this photo of boats in dry-dock in Bayfield, Wisconsin into an abstract interpretation of the subject.

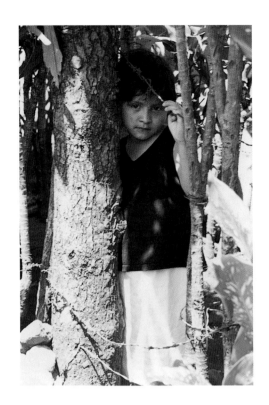

"Shooting from the hip" will provide you with spontaneous photos. Simply turn off the flash and aim your entire body at the subject and take a chance that you have him or her in your lens. Looking through a viewfinder is always a dead giveaway that you are taking a picture. I prefer to take pictures at this lower vantage point, especially at markets where the subjects are often stooped over or sitting. When photographing children, always stoop down to the same level as the child. Remember to respect the rights of your subjects, and if you plan to publicly display or sell your work, have them sign a model release.

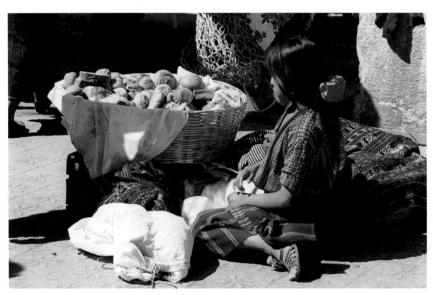

Use the **distance setting** (▲▲) when photographing through a window, placing the focus on the distance and not on the bus or car window. How often have you traveled by train, bus, ferry or car and seen inspiring subject matter out the window and known you would not be able to stop for a photo? By using a relatively fast film, such as 400 ASA, and setting your camera on ▲▲, you have a relatively good chance that your "window shots" will be successful.

My "spur-of-the-moment" photo of these women taken through a car window may provide an invaluable addition to a future painting.

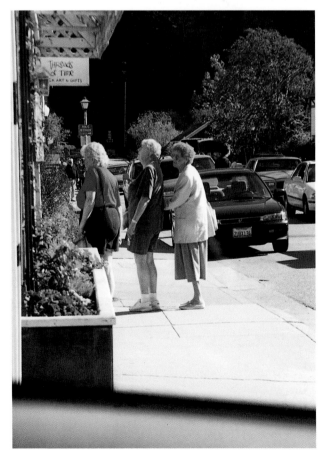

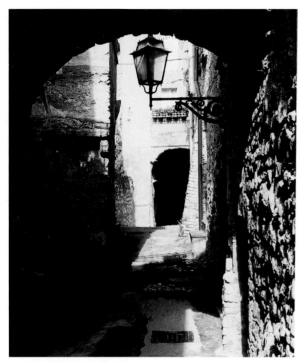

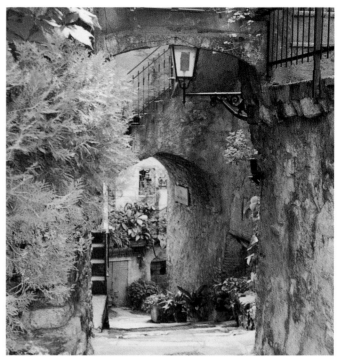

Without flash.

With flash.

Use a **fill-in flash** in full sunlight to soften and add detail to shadows. I took the photo on the left with my camera on automatic setting. I backed up a few feet and took a photo of the same subject using my fill-in flash. You may be surprised how the flash softens the subject, adds detail and reduces the contrast. A higher ASA film also helps to bridge the gap from

very dark to very light contrast. How many times have you looked forward to getting your photos back, only to be disappointed by the extreme dark and light contrasts? Photos taken in full sunlight often have no detail in the shadow. Try taking a photo using a fill-in flash and then try it without a flash.

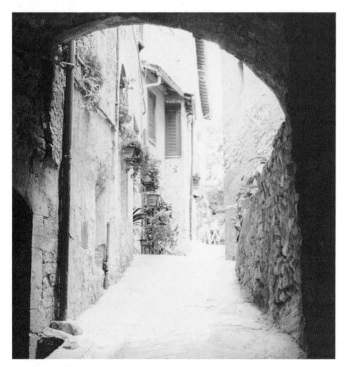

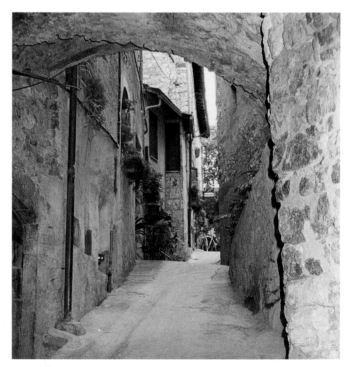

Without flash.

With flash.

Use a **fill-in flash** when you are in a dark place photographing into the light. These photos were taken under a medieval arch in Umbria, Italy, looking

out into the sun. The photo on the left has more artistic, dramatic impact, but the photo on the right is a better reference photo.

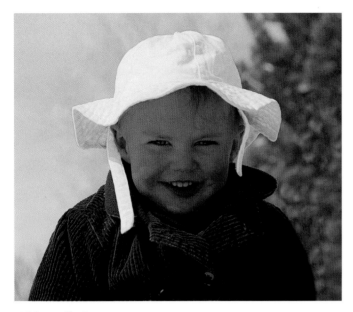

Without flash.

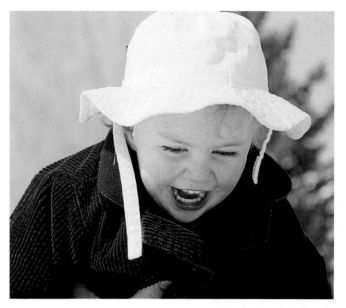

With flash.

Use a **fill-in flash** when photographing a subject under a large hat or umbrella to add more light to the shadow area. On the automatic setting of my camera, this photo of Rachael, wearing a wide-brimmed hat in full sun, did not engage the flash, and many of the details in her face are lost. The same subject, taken with a fill-in flash, gives detail to her face and softens the harsh shadows.

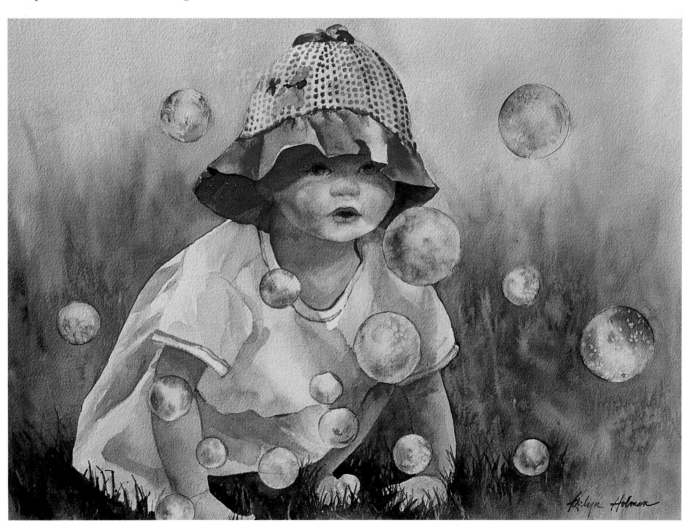

Children are natural subjects to photograph. Rachael's reaction to the bubbles provided endless painting material.

Illustrating children's picture books

Photographs are an indispensable aid when I illustrate children's picture books. It takes hundreds of drawings and endless research to find the right image. These images are designed to bring the story to life and breathe in character and mood and feelings. A children's picture book is short, and to visually capture the essence of the story is a challenge. All I have to work with is a writer's narrative.

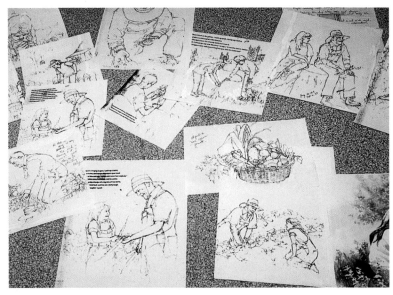

Planning a children's book usually means producing many drawings before finding the right image for the text. These are some of the preliminary drawings for *Grandpa's Garden*, Dawn Publications, 1996, by Shea Darian.

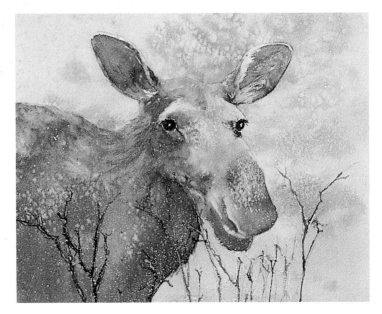

A curious moose from *Little Brother Moose*, Dawn Publications, 1995, by James Kasperson.

Brianna looking for a four-leaf clover from *Grandpa's Garden*, Dawn Publications, 1996, by Shea Darian.

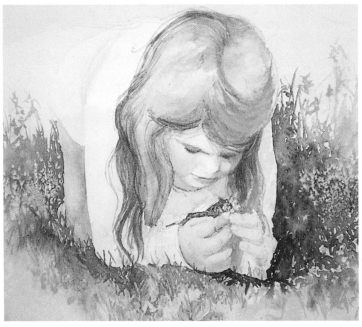

Using photographs in your studio

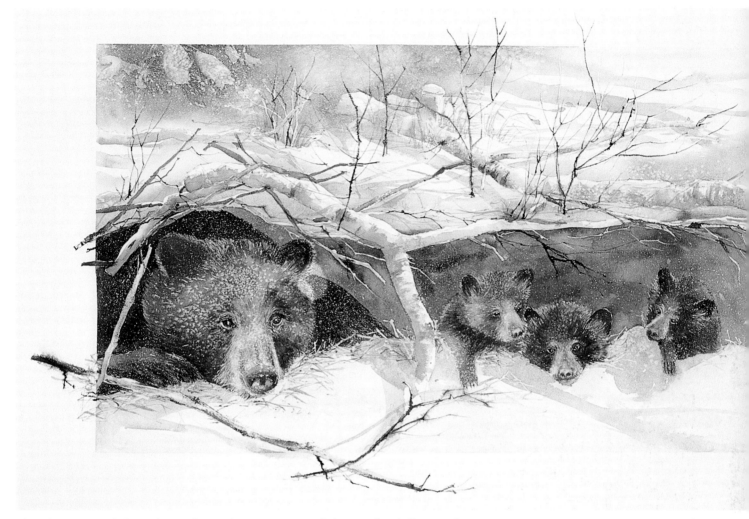

This illustration of sleepy bears from *Christmas Song of the North*, Pfeifer-Hamilton Publications, 1998, by Marsha Bonicatto, was composed using five different photographs, one for the background and one for each bear.

It is too easy to fall into the habit of copying a photograph when you paint. A photo should only be used as a starting point for your personal interpretation of the subject. Photographs distort color and value, everything is in focus, shadows are super hard-edged, and the color is almost always too blue. With the magic of watercolor, you can give real life and energy to your paintings using photographs as references. Photographic references can become a crutch, so use them only for study and research and then put them aside. Let the inspiration come from within to create your painting.

Using many photos as references, you can borrow elements from each to build a better composition. I prefer working with prints rather than slides because they are more flexible and portable.

Try going through old photos to find new compositions. Try vertical as well as horizontal formats. Your worst photos may inspire your best paintings. Sometimes I will go back to photos I took twenty years ago and see new possibilities when looking at them with a fresh eye. Look for old photos at thrift sales or in Grandma's attic. You never know where you may find your next inspiration.

Try taking double exposures

If you are not familiar with this technique, look for this symbol on your camera. ▭▪
Take the first picture. The film will not advance until you take the second picture.
Double exposures are fascinating and have inspired many of my paintings.

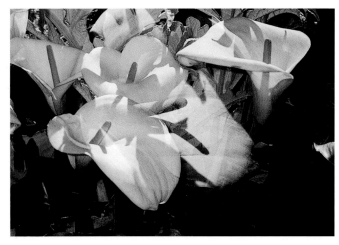

The calla lilies were superimposed over each other, one shot close up and the other at a distance.

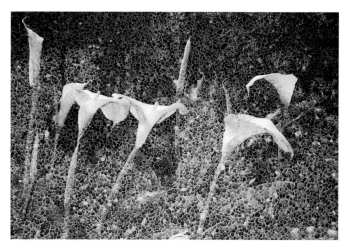

Here, the calla lilies were superimposed over a pebble driveway surface.

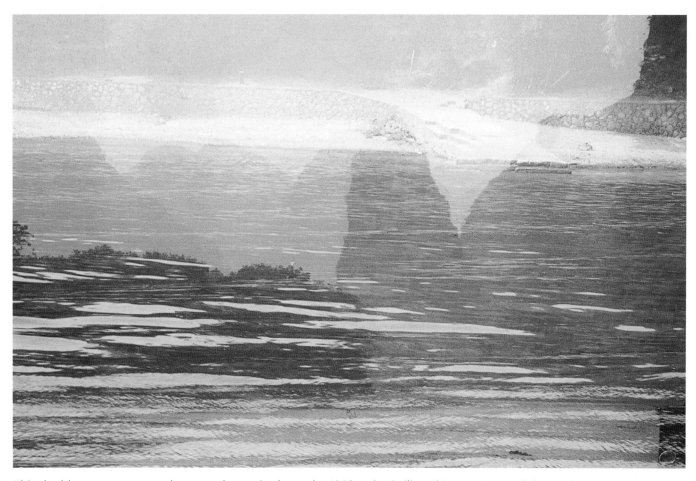

This double exposure was taken on a boat trip down the Li River in Guilin, China, 1996, and shows the shoreline superimposed over the "sugar loaf" mountains.

Using a Polaroid® SX-70 Camera

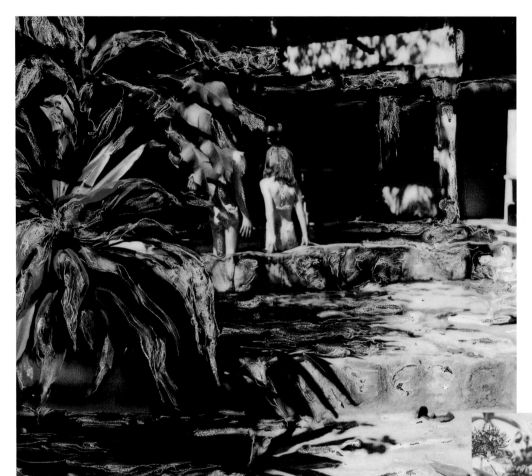

This SX-70 photo was taken in Playa del Carmen and manipulated with a plastic fork taken from my airline meal en route to the Yucatan. The photo was very dark, so by introducing more light shapes into the dark shapes, I created a more appealing subject.

This photo has blurry, nebulous shapes that could be the inspiration for an abstracted interpretation of this flower. The photo captured wonderful dark negative shapes that could enhance a painting.

The Polaroid® SX-70 Camera is a fun and inspirational camera which provides a simple and creative way to photograph and manipulate an image and has the added benefit of "instant results." This technique is becoming very popular and is sometimes referred to as **"painterly photography."** Unfortunately, this camera is difficult to find, but may be available at antique and thrift stores, yard sales or through internet trading. You simply take a picture with the SX-70 time zero film and, by manipulating the Polaroids (gels) layered inside, you can soften, blur and playfully change the image. For about one-half hour,

the chemicals remain soft, and with a tool, such as a plastic fork or toothpick, you can alter the image. You can edit out any extraneous details and you can even freeze an image to manipulate at a later time. To further enhance the image, you can paint on the photographs with oil paints. You can also enlarge the images on a color copier and print them on transfer sheets that can then be transferred to heavy watercolor paper. Many artists are turning this film medium into impressionistic art. These exciting techniques and ideas are being shared on the Internet.

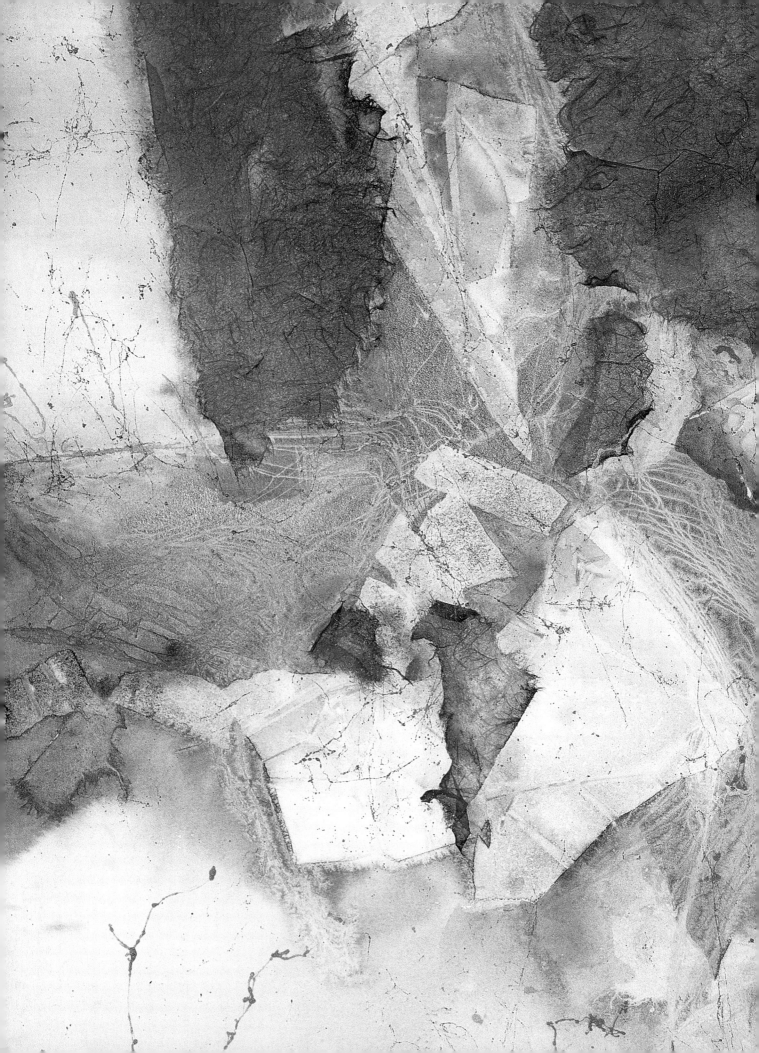

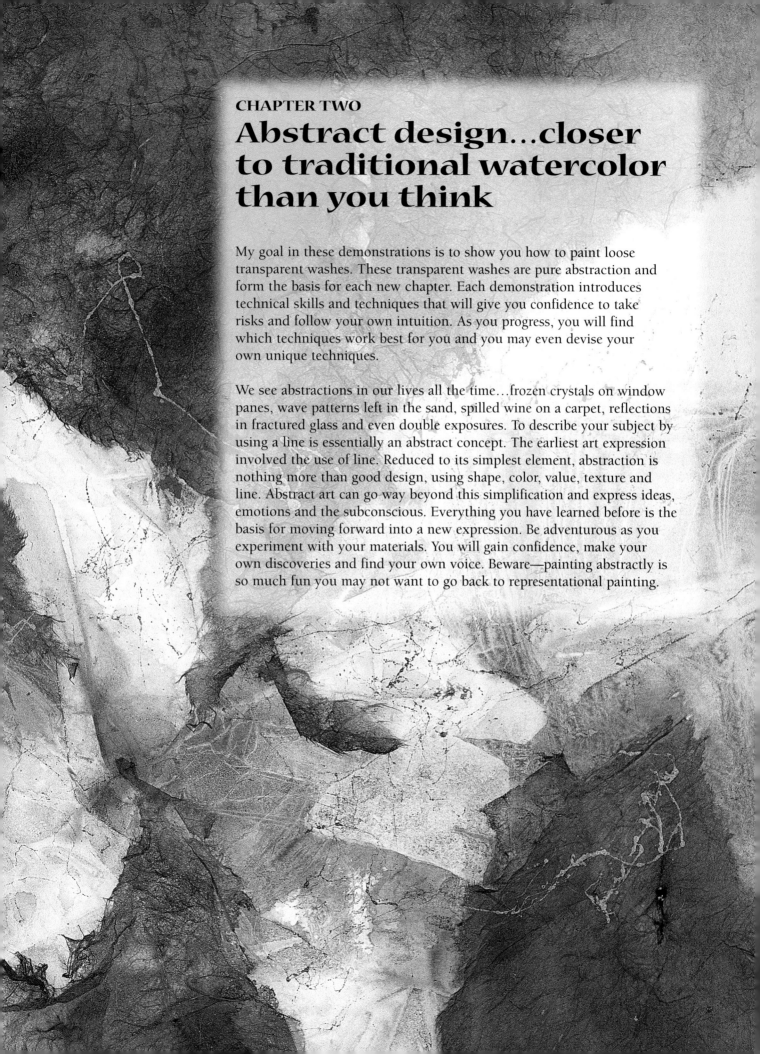

CHAPTER TWO
Abstract design...closer to traditional watercolor than you think

My goal in these demonstrations is to show you how to paint loose transparent washes. These transparent washes are pure abstraction and form the basis for each new chapter. Each demonstration introduces technical skills and techniques that will give you confidence to take risks and follow your own intuition. As you progress, you will find which techniques work best for you and you may even devise your own unique techniques.

We see abstractions in our lives all the time...frozen crystals on window panes, wave patterns left in the sand, spilled wine on a carpet, reflections in fractured glass and even double exposures. To describe your subject by using a line is essentially an abstract concept. The earliest art expression involved the use of line. Reduced to its simplest element, abstraction is nothing more than good design, using shape, color, value, texture and line. Abstract art can go way beyond this simplification and express ideas, emotions and the subconscious. Everything you have learned before is the basis for moving forward into a new expression. Be adventurous as you experiment with your materials. You will gain confidence, make your own discoveries and find your own voice. Beware—painting abstractly is so much fun you may not want to go back to representational painting.

Developing an adventurous attitude

Whether you work figuratively, abstractly or realistically, you are working with design relationships. Regardless of what the subject is or how it is painted, the same concerns are an integral part of the success of a painting. The shapes, values, color, directional movement, lines, and the elements of good design are what make a painting work. This chapter is devoted to working with universal design elements and experimental techniques. I always start my classes with free-flowing, spontaneous lessons that focus on color and design, rather than on traditional drawing and painting techniques. My students produce extraordinary works during these lessons.

My art training was loosely based on abstract expressionism. I see paintings in black and white shapes, so values and shapes come easily for me. I see these shapes in traditional as well as non-representational paintings. This is why I feel working non-objectively is a valuable design experience. You can train yourself to evaluate a painting purely from its abstract design qualities. Whether a subject is rendered realistically or abstractly, both paintings share the same design elements.

My goal in this chapter is to give you some rules and technical tools to guide you in this process. My greatest hope is that you will take risks and follow your own intuition, and as you progress, you will make your own rules. Determine what works for you and remember—you are unique and only you can present your point of view in your special way. All you really need is a "spirit of adventure."

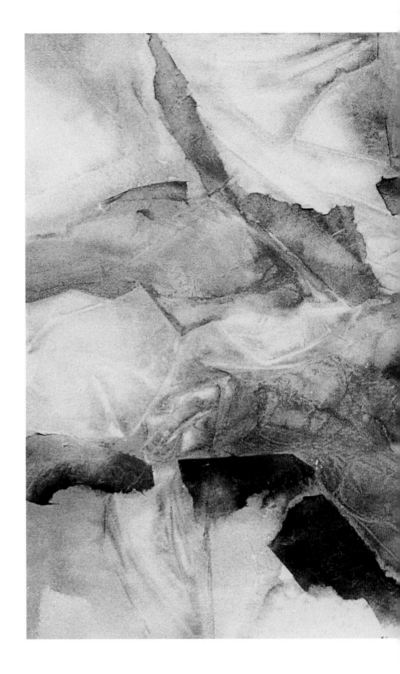

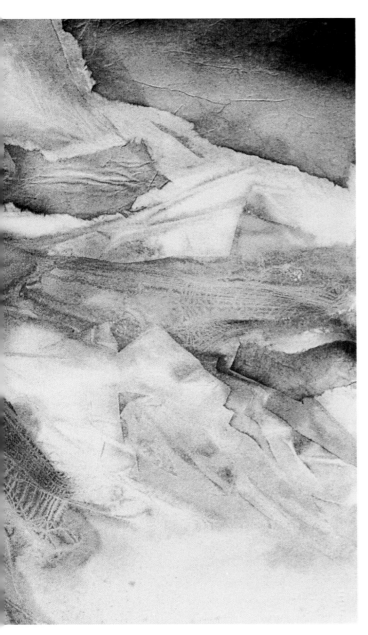
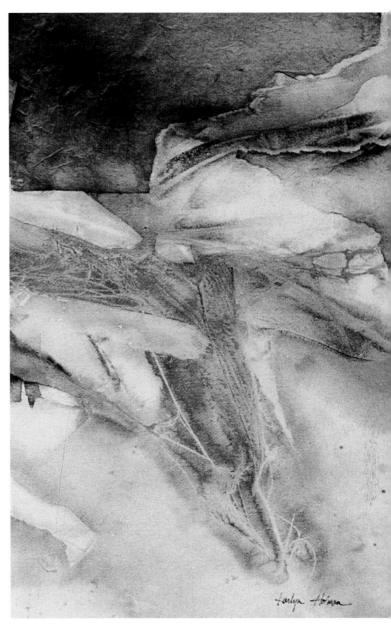

This is a diptych titled WINTER NEGATIVE. When you paint a diptych, paint both sections at once so the colors and movement flow together. Place the papers side by side, allowing enough space between the two papers for any matting and framing that is necessary. If you butt the papers together at the time you are painting the picture, the lines of movement will not work together after the painting is framed.

Non-objective…fun and free approach to pure design

The first lesson involves non-objective painting. Color, value, texture and movement are the major elements in this lesson. We will experiment with many techniques, always keeping design uppermost in our minds. Understanding good design will put an underlying abstract design in all your subjects. Try to open your mind and heart and let things happen without too many preconceived hopes of what the finished painting will look like. Open the door and experience the joy of a new form of expression. This experimental, risk-taking approach often leads to the creation of a painting based on your emotional response to the materials, instead of on draftsmanship and representational accuracy. You can free yourself from trying to make the painting look like something and just enjoy the texture, movement and color.

This demonstration will focus on guiding you through a process of self-discovery using only a few simple textural design elements. Work quickly and do not even think about control. Think of yourself as an observer just watching the paint discover its own path.

Any paper will work for this approach. I chose 260# Winsor Newton because of its whiteness and absorbency. Do not soak and stretch your paper because this process floats away the sizing. Simply wet the paper, and as you introduce the color, let it float on the sizing. This mixture of sizing and color moves about freely and lifts easily.

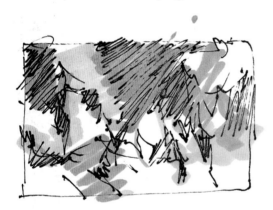

Start with a few **thumbnail sketches** to design a pattern of movement and dark and light shapes. Use these as references, but do not draw any pencil lines on your painting paper. Looking at your sketches, apply color wet-into-wet onto the paper. Be sure you use rich mixtures of color. If the color looks too rich when it is wet, it will be just right when it dries. Because color loses a great deal of value when it dries, always work with a generous amount of paint. After the initial wet-into-wet start, you can start thinking about control. Think about directional movement and connecting shapes as you apply the paint.

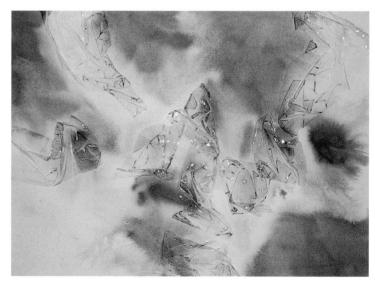

Color. Use harmonic color to start the wet-into-wet wash. When applying the color, always remember to save *white or light shapes.*

An abstract painting can be the most exciting "accident on purpose." For the most part, you are in control, but many wonderful things happen by accident. The traditional tool for watercolor is the brush, but there are many other tools you can experiment with, such as wax paper, plastic wrap, salt, gauze and collage. These materials are not merely "gimmicks." They all provide interesting textural effects that a brush can not produce.

Line. Line can be achieved by using gauze. The gauze is easily ripped and stretched and is laid directly onto the wet paper to form lines. If the gauze touches color, it will absorb it.

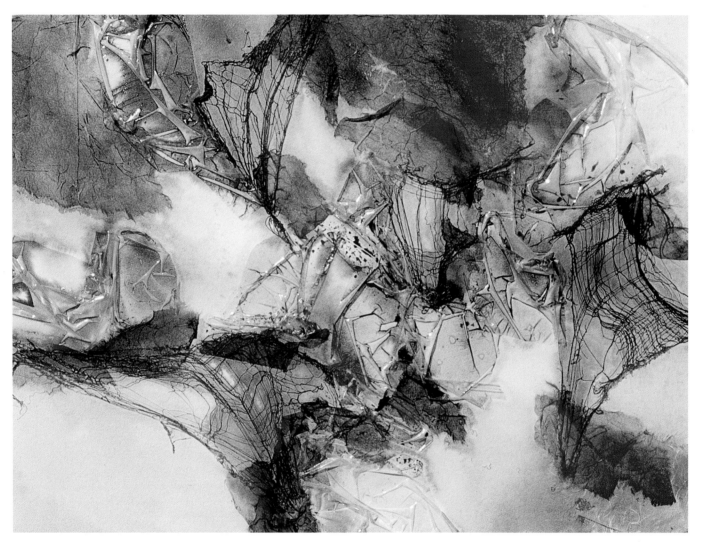

Light shapes. Put plastic wrap or wax paper on the white shapes that you have saved. The plastic wrap or wax paper will create texture and help save these areas as white shapes.

Dark shapes. Creating dark shapes is the easiest part. If you use Thai, white unryu oriental paper, you will find that this unsized, archival paper absorbs the paint and forms the darks. This precious paper is your ticket to a successful painting. Be generous with the application of unryu paper because it can be moved around and used to cover any unwanted textures later.

Spray metallic paint in selected areas while the painting is still wet. Most artists think they want to skip this part, but this spray produces crisp "stencil" shapes and gives the painting a unified look. Gold and silver always work well, but sometimes a designer color adds the perfect touch. My latest addition is "webbing spray" which produces a wonderful scribbly line that would be impossible to create on your own—another "accident on purpose" style of line.

When the paint dries, you can look at your work objectively and decide if it needs further development. Be very careful not to undo the essence of what you just expressed. Painting wet-into-wet is very different from adding marks to the painting after it dries. Know when to stop and do not go too far—less can be more.

When you find yourself more interested in the color, textures and movement of the paint, you are opening up your soul to the abstract world. Instead of trying to paint something recognizable, simply let the pure colors mix on the surface, watch the textures happen, and enjoy the spontaneity. This way of painting allows you to express your feelings in a non-representational way.

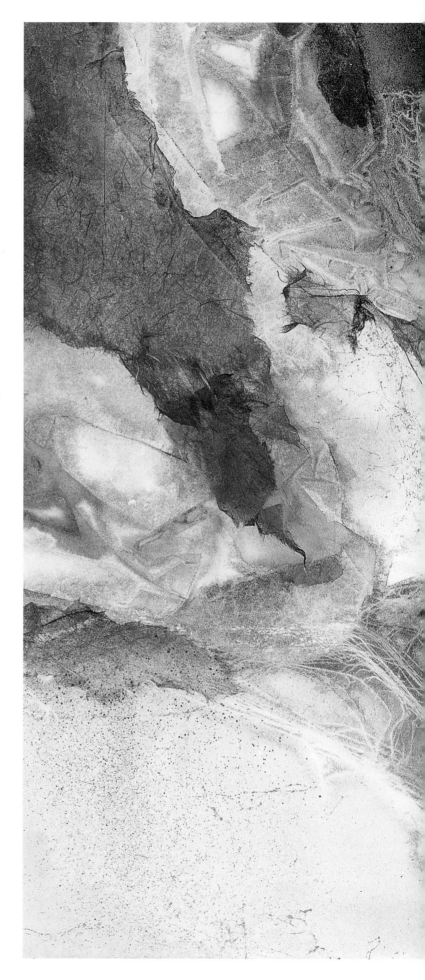

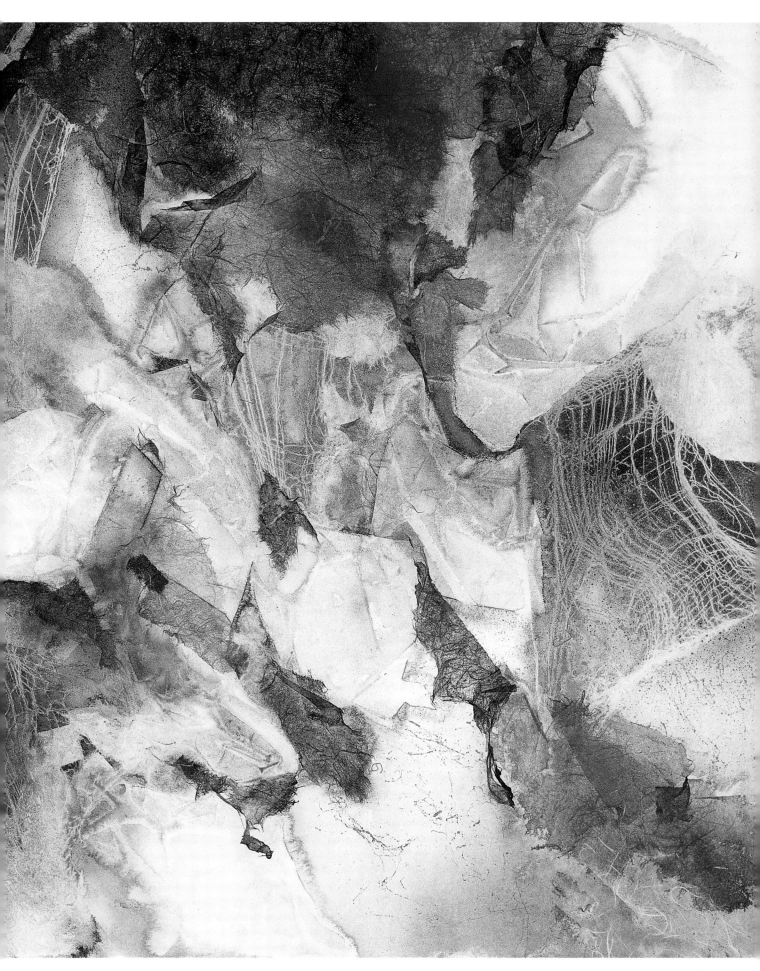

Collage...a movable feast

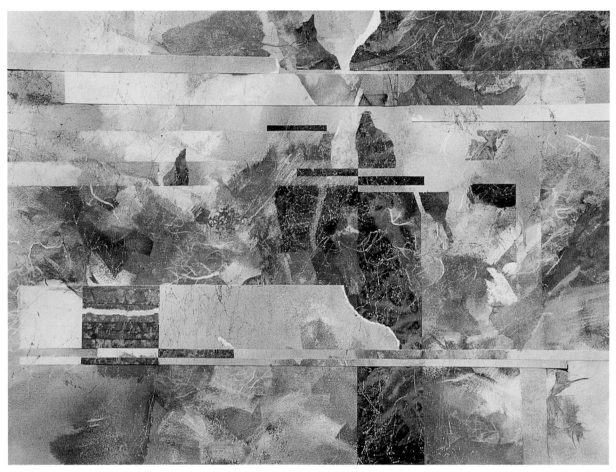

Collage is a great way to simplify shapes, manipulate color, have fun with texture and achieve dynamic and unique results. For the abstract artist, this movable feast is a popular way to work because you can try out colors or shapes and move them around until you are pleased with your composition. Collage is also a very forgiving medium because it allows you to decide ahead of time how you want the picture to look. I am working non-objectively in this demonstration, but the subject matter could be representational. The possibilities are limitless in collage. Many fine artists are making portraits, still lifes, landscapes, etc., using this technique.

An "old dog" is one of my paintings that I have really tried to make into a "frameable" painting, with little success. These are paintings that are too light, too bright, too dark or too lacking in design or magic. I used to ask students to bring in their "old dogs" so we could use them for raw material for collages. One artist who did not understand this concept was so conscientious that she brought in thirty-six photographs of old dogs, and another artist actually did a painting of an old dog. Now, in my workshops, I always make sure I define the term "old dogs" accurately.

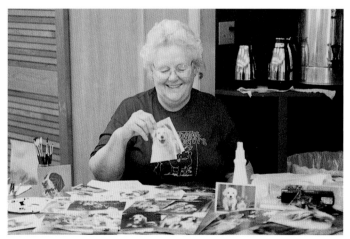

Bea with her collection of "old dog" photos. Bea had to sign an affidavit swearing she would return some of these photos before people agreed to let her use them.

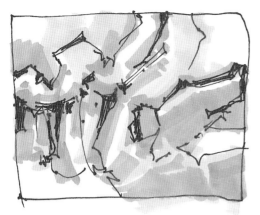

Thumbnail sketch.

Begin the painting with an "old dog" or any kind of archival papers that excite you. I have always been fascinated with lightweight oriental papers because I respond emotionally to their fibered textures and colors.

Arrange the papers into a design, keeping in mind directional movement and variations in size. Using this approach, you first will create dark values and save light values. Be sure to remember to leave connecting white areas throughout the composition. The word collage means "to paste." Once you have arranged your design, paste down the papers with the appropriate glue. For 140# paper or heavier, use a thick glue which can be applied to the back of the paper, such as "Yes," Sobo™, Aleene's® Thick Designer Glue or Elmer's® Glue-all™. For lightweight oriental papers, use matte medium and varnish mixed half and half with water and apply this mixture directly on top of the papers. This mixture penetrates the unryu and bonds itself to the surface. Always use inexpensive brushes to apply the glue.

After the papers dry, rewet the entire piece and add wet-into-wet colors. Choose harmonic colors to enrich and enliven the colors already in the collage materials.

If you want more texture, you can use unryu (darks), gauze (line), or plastic wrap (lights).

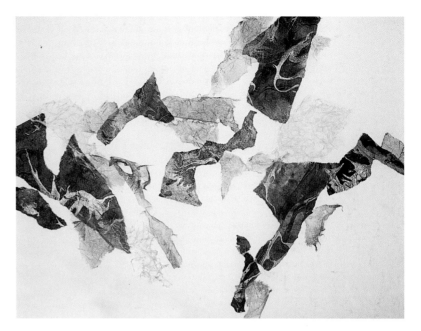

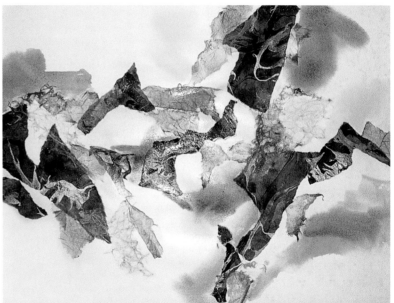

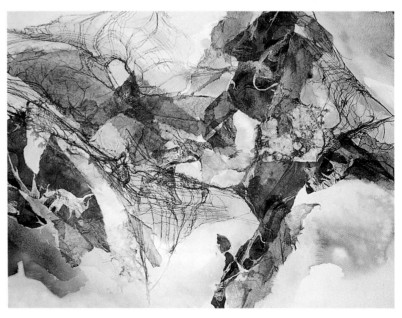

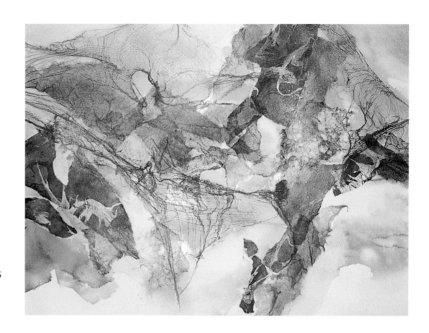

Spray metallic paint while the surface is still wet.

After the painting is dry, continue to paint if your painting needs darks or more intense color. I added more bright colors and some white unryu to soften some of the transitions.

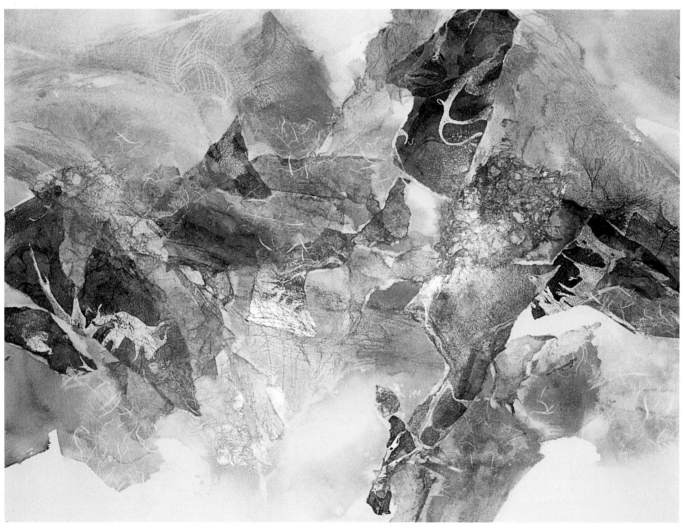

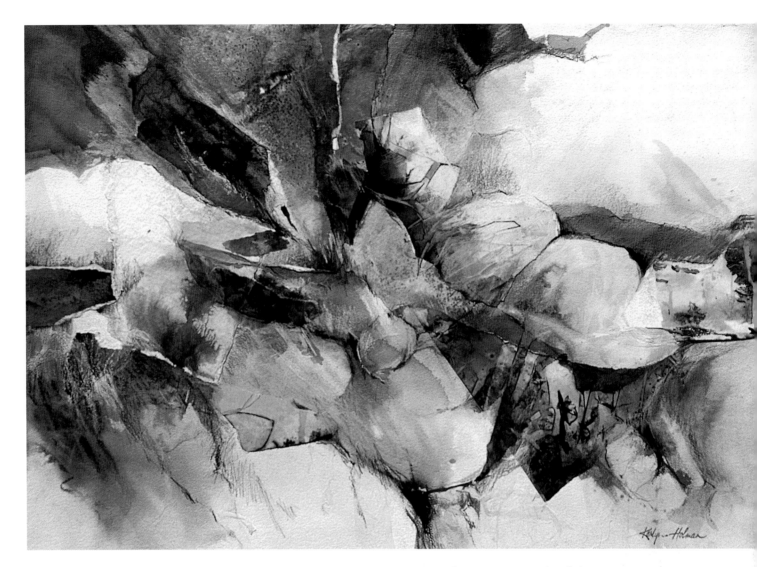

On this painting, I glued down 140# paper and intentionally ripped the paper so the white edges became part of the design. Pencil and colored pencil lines were added for further enhancement. **Water-soluble colored pencils** make you feel as though you are drawing and painting at the same time. Using this technique brings back memories. Remember those water-activated coloring books you had when you were a child?

Weaving…adding a new dimension

On your journey as an artist, you often come to a point when you need to experiment with a new form of expression and go beyond the confines of traditional watercolor. Weaving papers together is a technique I often use. Sometimes I am not sure whether the resulting works are paintings or weavings. If your desire to experiment can be enhanced by using weaving, give yourself permission to give it a try.

Painting a picture can be like **weaving**. I frequently paint a picture as if I am weaving the paint over and under shapes. Actually weaving with paper is a natural outgrowth of this painting technique and adds an interesting dimension to your work.

Select papers of contrasting colors. If this is your first attempt at weaving, use a basic tabby weave—over and under one strip at a time—making the colors appear and disappear. To break up the monotony of this equal pattern, try tearing some of the paper to make irregular shapes. These purple and yellow paintings were not exciting on their own, but woven together, they became more of a statement. The positives and negatives reverse when they are combined.

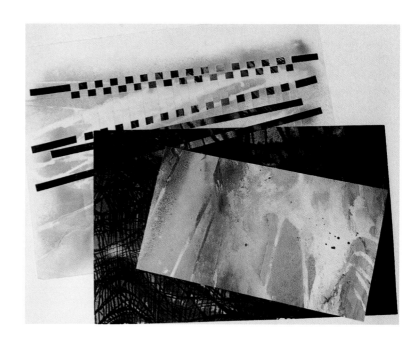

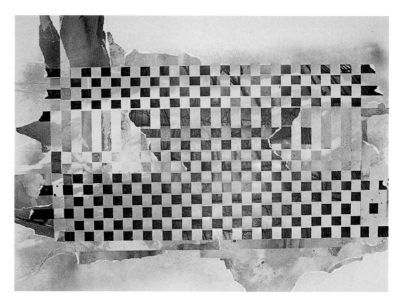

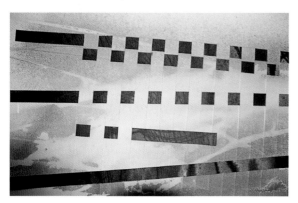

Cut the paper only in the area that you plan to weave.

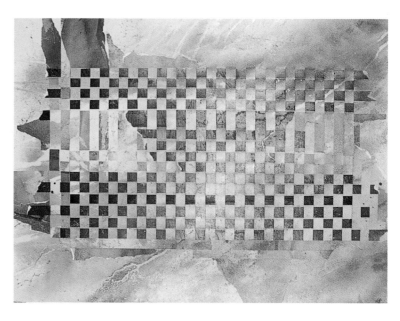

The strips of the finished woven piece were glued in place and gold and purple metallic sprays were used to add the finishing touch.

46

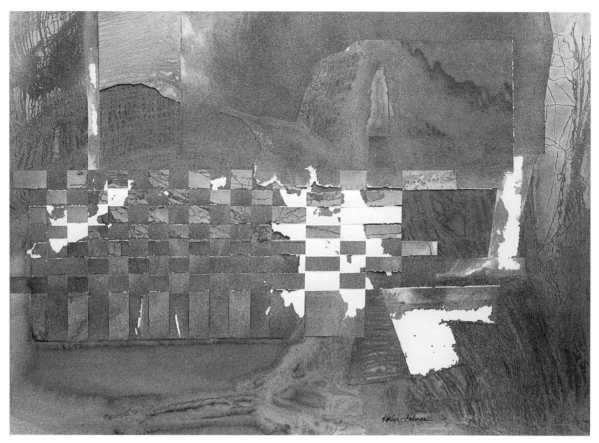

Sometimes a painting needs to be combined with another painting to really become an entity. This woven piece started out as a diptych but lacked visual impact. I used one piece of the diptych as the background and cut and wove in sections from the other piece to create the finished work. Originally published in *In Harmony with Nature* by Maxine Masterfield, Watson-Guptill Publications, 1990.

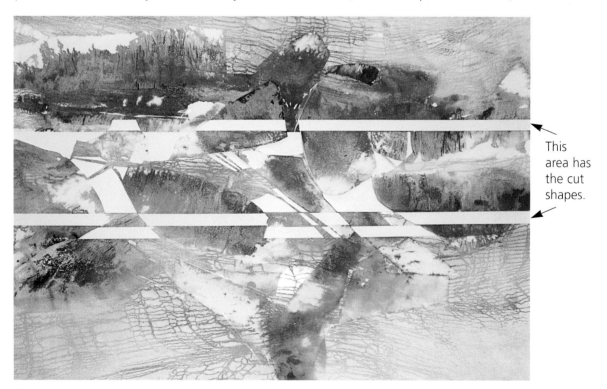

This area has the cut shapes.

This painting needed whites to pull the composition together. First, I determined the areas that needed to be strengthened in the painting and cut these areas away with an X-acto® knife, gluing white paper underneath to fill in the shapes. Then I cut and wove in the additional horizontal white strips.

Semi-abstracting...capturing the essence of recognizable subjects

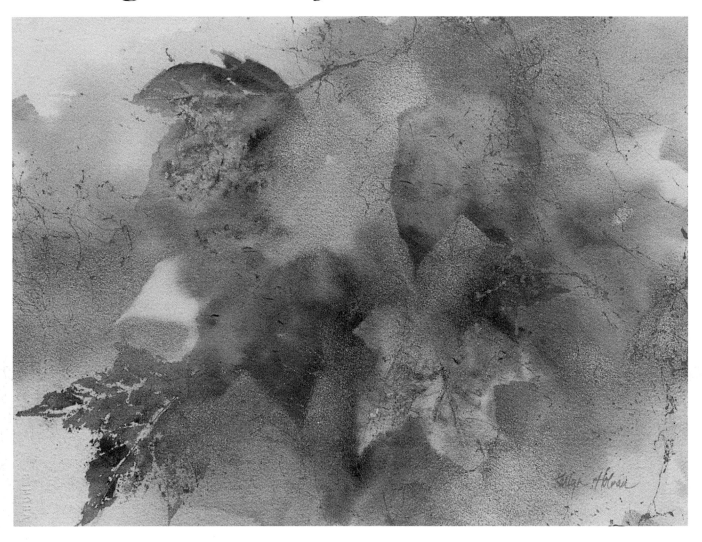

My love for realism, mixed with my love for abstraction, come together in this lesson. Semi-abstraction has more appeal to me than absolute realism or total non-objective painting. My instinct to paint realistically, combined with my knowledge of basic design principles, makes achieving this balance possible. If I see my painting moving too closely toward realism, I concentrate more on design. If my painting is becoming too non-objective, I look for recognizable elements to bring it back to a comfortable balance. One of the easiest ways to see abstractly is to view your subject in **close focus**. Many artists employ this technique because this myopic way of looking at a subject really helps them see abstract shapes. The work of Georgia O'Keefe is an outstanding example of the use of this technique.

To begin, study your subject and decide on the shapes, colors and textures you want to use in your painting. Some parts of the subject may be painted more realistically and others may be more abstracted. Push and pull the tension to arrive at a semi-abstract interpretation.

Process. This approach may be more exciting if you do not do a preliminary sketch. Any paper will work for this lesson. Winsor Newton is a good choice because it is a whiter paper and the colors will look more vibrant. Wet both sides of the paper so it will lie flat and give you a longer working time. When applying the colors, think about the shapes and move your brush, keeping **directional movement** in mind. Use **analogous** colors at this early stage. Apply only pure color so the paint will mix on the paper and not on your palette. Remember to save your whites.

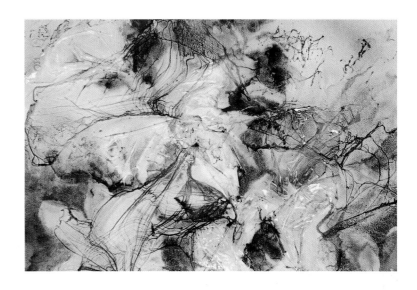

After the harmonic colors become acquainted, think about **contrast**. Placing complementary or cool colors in the background will make the painting more exciting visually. Strive for a variety of textures and shapes, lost and found edges, and as much contrast as possible.

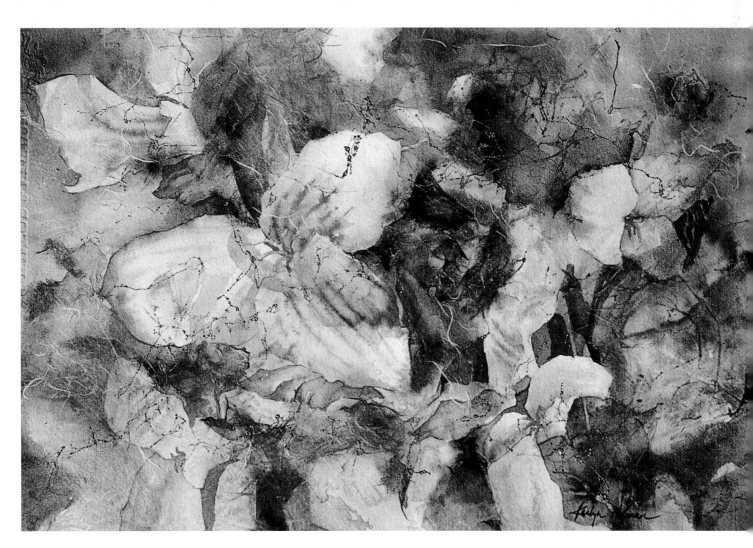

Semi-abstracted landscapes

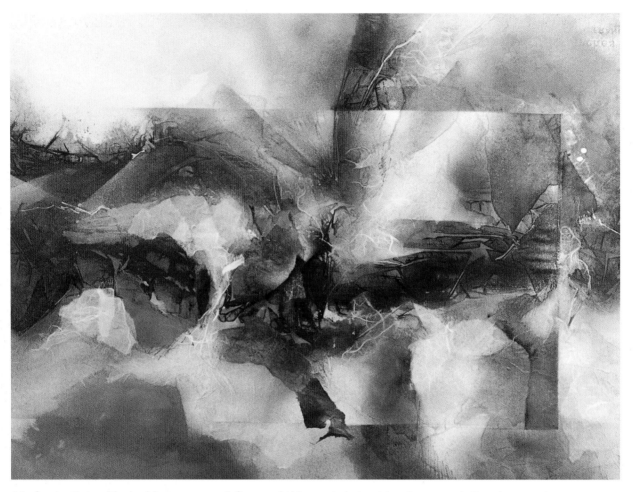

My fascination with double exposures influenced this semi-abstract landscape painting. I sprayed white ink and glued down white unryu paper to provide soft transitional areas between the dark and mid-tone colors.

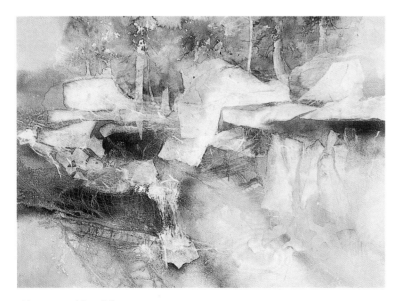

Abstracted land form.

The Lake Superior sandstone shorelines near my home provide a wealth of material to use as a departure point for creating an abstracted landscape. These rocks and trees along the shoreline suggest many geometric and light and dark patterns. When you paint a semi-abstracted landscape, you need not worry about perspective. Simply vary the sizes of the shapes and overlap some shapes to give a feeling of depth. Cluster or group some shapes to create a focal point and design some out-of-focus rest areas to complete the composition. You may find it difficult to leave certain elements out of the painting, but semi-abstraction is achieved by simplifying the subject. As you learn to use this approach, you will find it easier to leave out non-essential details and focus on expressing the ideas—**evaluate, select and simplify**.

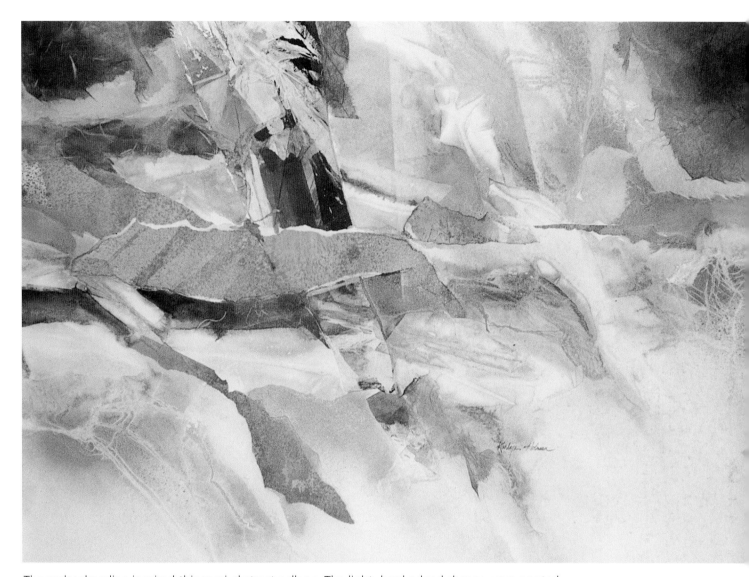

The rocky shoreline inspired this semi-abstract collage. The light, hard-edged shapes were created by using a damp sponge and a piece of plastic. The color was lifted in crisp, directional shapes to add variety and movement.

Close focus imagery

Colorful leaves in ditches or rocks in pools of water are appealing subjects to paint. The strong negative patterns help you focus on painting around the shapes rather than painting the positive shapes themselves. If you want to improve your negative painting skills, try using this close-up viewpoint.

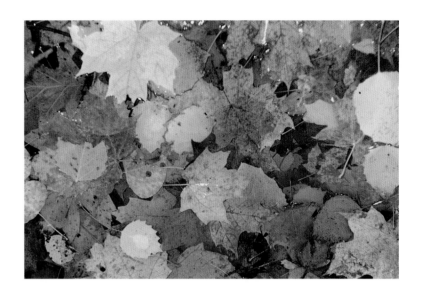

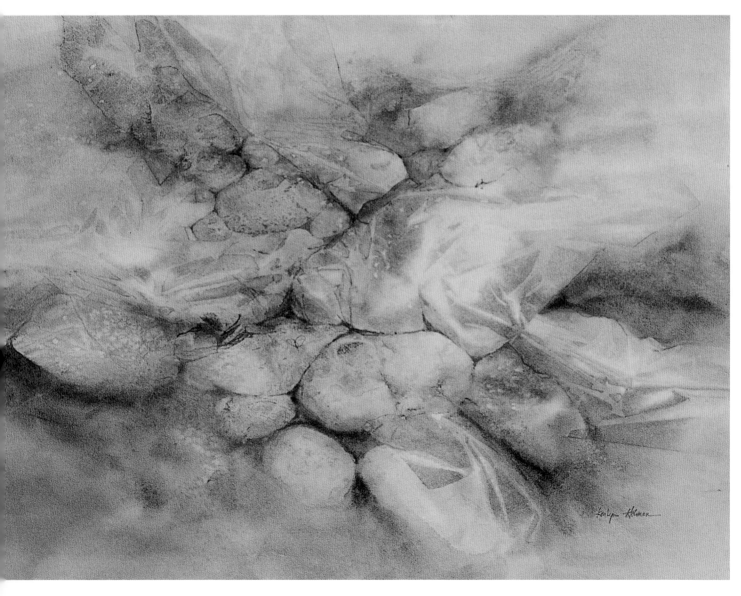

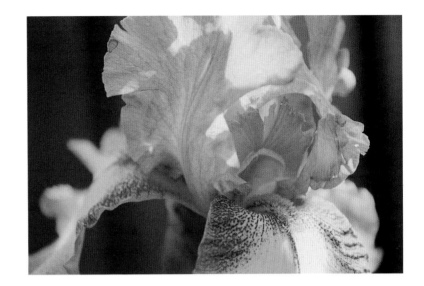

The colors, movement and shapes in the photo inspired this semi-abstract painting of an iris. The painting was created with no pre-drawing, using wet-into-wet color application. Only a few layered colors were added after the painting dried.

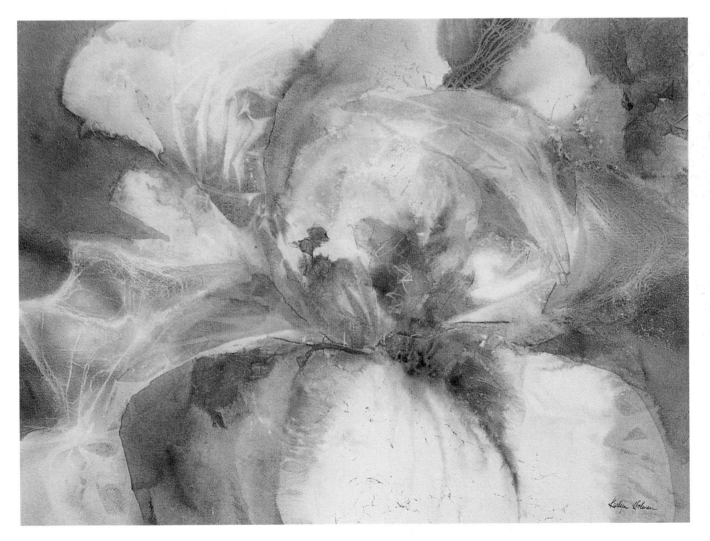

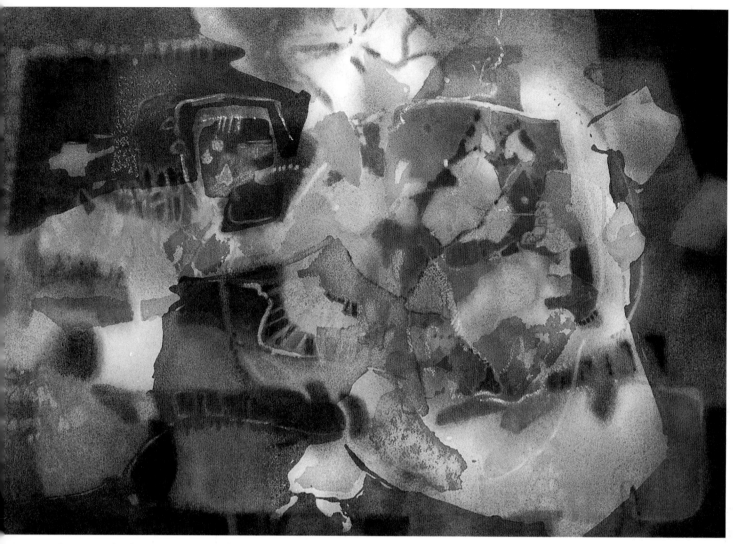

Susan Luzier is a master at working in a semi-abstract approach.
She layers many washes until her subject emerges out of the soft
edges, as in this painting titled LA HAUTE CUISINE.

*"Sometimes when I work in the abstract the image reveals itself
to me with the first wash. Such was the case with LA HAUTE
CUISINE. Four white napkins and the table for four jumped out
at me. All I had to do was add a menu of shapes, values and
textures. Bon appétit."* —Susan Luzier

Fibered unryu over an "old dog"...a way to save a painting

Many times a painting just does not work. Many of my paintings have potential, but lack that final resolve. I look at these paintings as an exciting challenge to try something innovative. Do they need to be simplified by glazing? Would layering collage papers on them help develop a focal point? Could they be cut into a smaller format? Would adding darks help? I feel that putting the energy into saving a painting is a worthwhile learning experience.

One of the techniques that really works for me is to place and glue 10-gram fibered Thai white unryu paper, **fiber side up**, over the entire painting. This technique subdues and softens the subject. Use a mixture of half water and half matte medium and varnish to adhere the paper to the painting. Start in the center of the painting and place glue on top of the paper and brush in a circular motion out to the edges. As you glue, the paper will stretch, so move slowly and carefully and do not trap any air bubbles. After the glue dries, you may continue to paint. The paint will lie on the surface and if you do not like the results, you can wipe the paint off. When you are pleased with the results, simply allow the paint to dry.

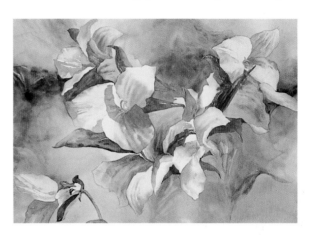

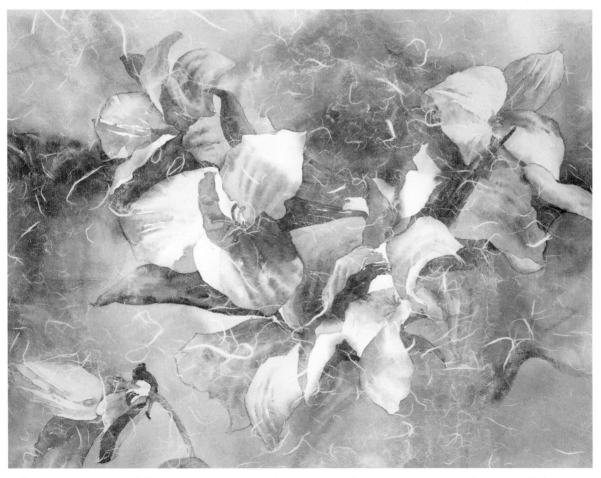

Trilliums are a protected flower in Wisconsin and a sure sign of spring. This painting became a little dark and hard-edged and was enhanced by the softness of the fibered paper.

I have always looked at a less-than-inspiring painting as an opportunity…a springboard to new ideas. Many artists insist that watercolor is impossible to correct and that every brushstroke must count, but this is not necessarily true. I am constantly surprised at how much I can change. Did you know you can actually scrub away the color on a watercolor painting? Armed with only a toothbrush and running water, you can wash out just about anything, and if you are not too aggressive, you can actually repaint the same surface. Try to breathe new life into a less-than-exciting painting by pulling out all the artillery—brayers, opaque paint, glue, colored pencils—whatever you can think of. Much of what I have learned about painting has resulted from trying to salvage my "old dogs." When you have nothing to lose, you are more willing to take risks and experiment, and all kinds of exciting things can happen.

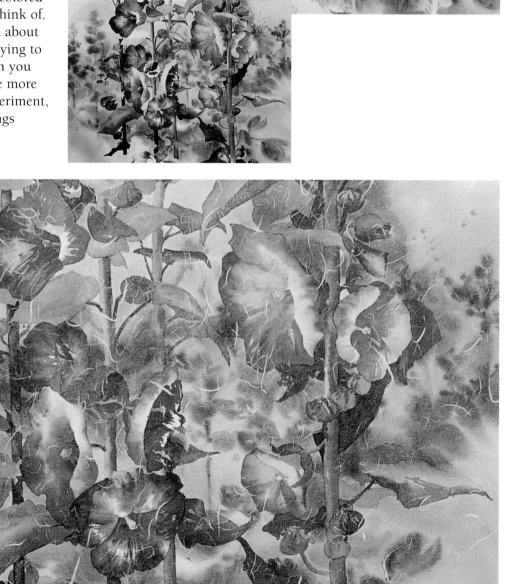

This painting started with a wet-into-wet underpainting, then the hollyhocks were painted on dry paper. The unryu softened the background, subdued the dark shapes, and focused more attention on the hollyhocks.

Cardstock and jewelry...the ultimate "old dog!"

When I have tried everything in my bag of tricks and I cannot make that element of magic appear, I use the painting for cards, mini-paintings and jewelry. At this point, I can be free at last—no longer held hostage by my unfinished paintings. While I am cutting up my paintings, I feel reborn, ready to move on to another adventure.

"Old dog" jewelry has been a profitable, as well as fun way to put my uninteresting paintings to rest. You can glue the watercolor image to leftover matboard and make pins, earrings, necklaces, etc. The finish is a liquid plastic coating that is poured over the surface and hardens into a glossy finish. One coat is equal to fifty coats of varnish. This mixture of a hardener and an epoxy can be purchased at any craft store. Envirotex Lite™ or Ultra-Glo™ are two of the popular brand names. Just follow the directions on the package.

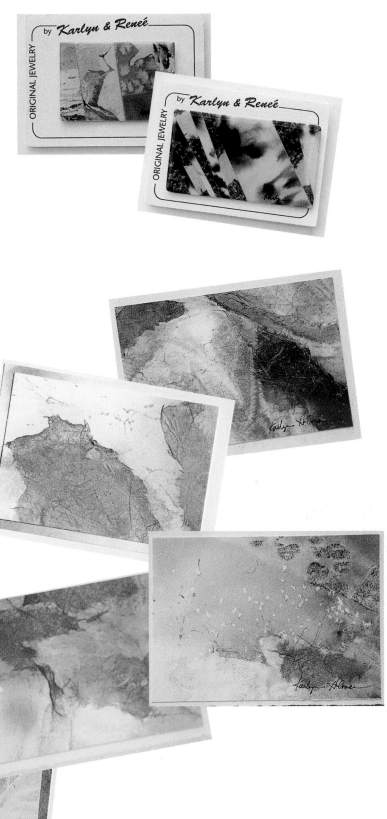

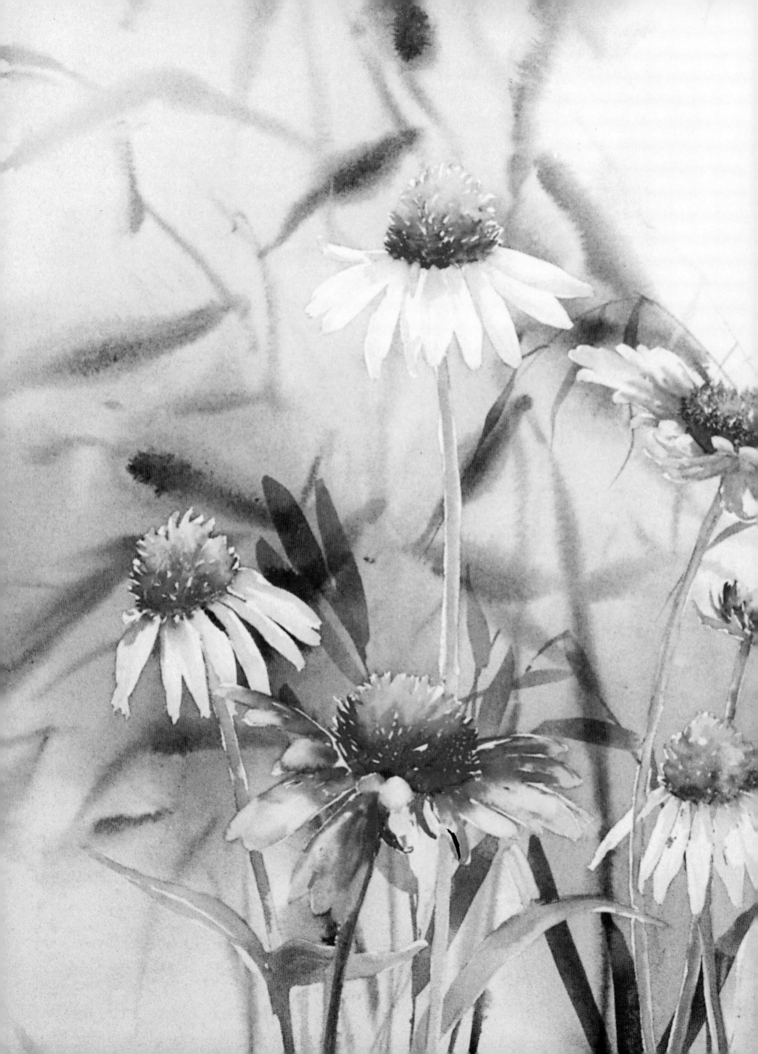

CHAPTER THREE
Floral design...celebrating color

The fun and free washes in your pure abstractions are now going to become the mid-tone dark patterns in your floral backgrounds.

The following three demonstrations are designed as step-by-step concepts and techniques that are tools to enable you to paint whatever you choose in your own personal style. When you do not understand a technique, or the process, or basic composition, you can easily find yourself discouraged. These lessons are described in an easy-to-follow outline to give you the information you need for your own departure.

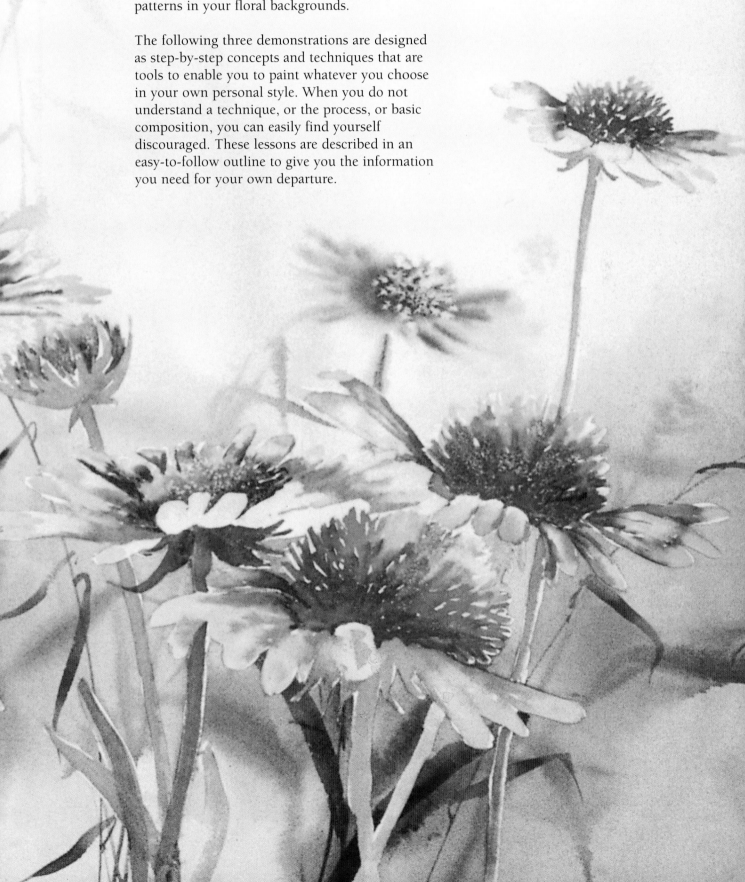

Wet-into-wet background first... starting your painting with an exciting background of color and value

This approach starts with a wet-into-wet background wash using pure color. Before the color dries, out-of-focus flowers and shapes are added. I love this approach because it is so direct. In this type of painting, you can actually complete most of the painting in the first wash. You may feel like you are putting together a jigsaw puzzle, but eventually all the pieces fall into place.

This lesson is a perfect example of the benefits of planning ahead. The success of the painting depends in large part on the composition. The drawing is as much fun to conceive as it is to paint.

As you draw the flowers, think about the following considerations:

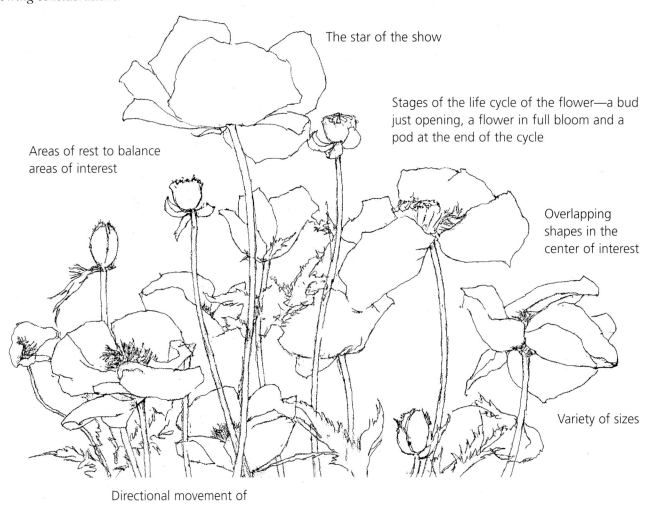

The star of the show

Stages of the life cycle of the flower—a bud just opening, a flower in full bloom and a pod at the end of the cycle

Areas of rest to balance areas of interest

Overlapping shapes in the center of interest

Variety of sizes

Directional movement of the chorus

When drawing in the shapes, concentrate on the contours, the thickness of the stems, and the overlapping of the shapes.

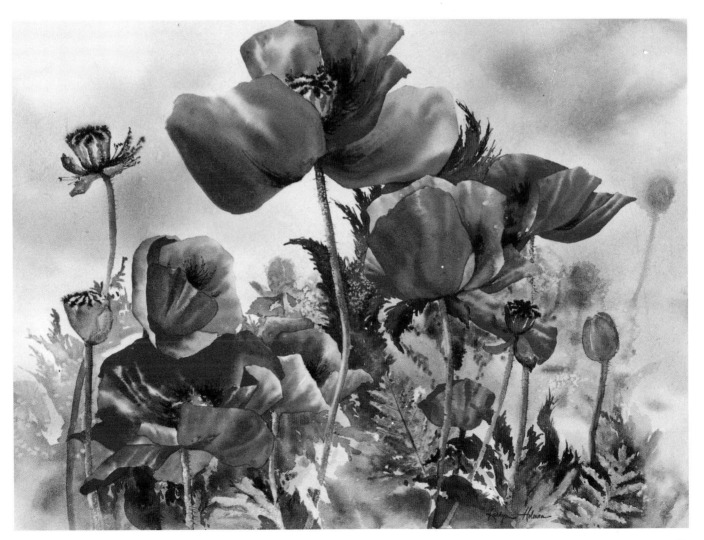

When you **compose** your painting, you usually start by deciding on a vertical or horizontal format. The vertical format on the right has very restful, subtle lights in the background. The horizontal format I chose for this demonstration has a more dramatic background with more abstract qualities.

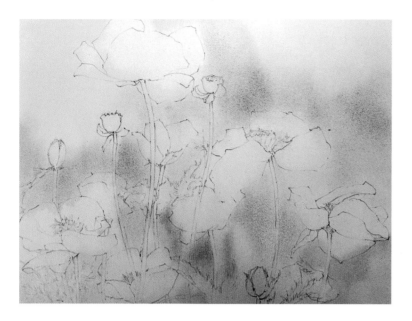

Background wash. For this style of painting, use 140# cold press Arches paper because it is more forgiving. Cold press allows washes to blend together and has fewer bleed-backs. Wet both sides of the paper until it is totally saturated. Really soak the paper to give yourself the longest possible working time. You may also put the paper on a non-porous surface to keep it wet longer. You want as much control as possible, but you also want to stay loose as long as possible. Paint everything except the drawn flowers and enjoy the colors as they float around in the water. Your biggest challenge will be to **save the whites** in your interest area. Later these areas will be a color (such as the red poppies in this demonstration).

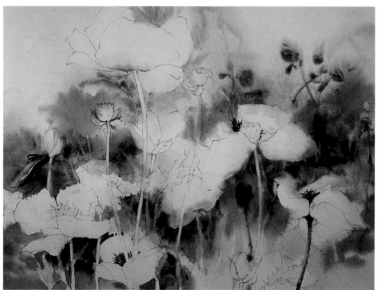

Design a pattern of **mid-tone dark values** around the pre-drawn shapes. This background wash is very similar to the technique used in non-objective painting. Do not paint anything you drew. Remember, everything will look out of focus. Do not worry about color that bleeds into the flower shapes. This color later becomes the shadows. In my painting, the green background becomes neutralized by the red poppies.

Keep some areas **restful** for contrast.
Add **shadow images** of flowers.
Add **out-of-focus shapes**.

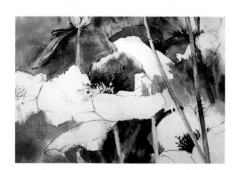

When the paper has fully dried, paint each flower petal, one by one. Wet one petal at a time and apply pure color. In this demonstration, I applied pure Winsor yellow, permanent rose and scarlet lake into each wet shape. As the colors are getting acquainted, tip the paper so the colors will mix more easily. Really try to save whites or lights within these shapes to maintain the illusion of light reflecting off the flowers.

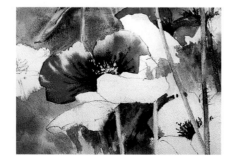

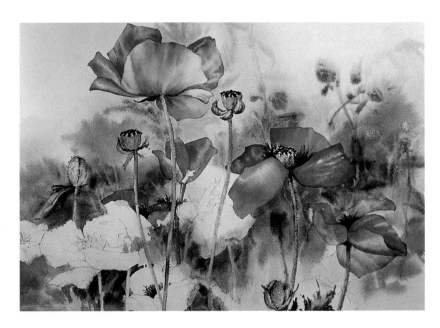

Finishing the painting is like putting a jigsaw puzzle together, one piece at a time.

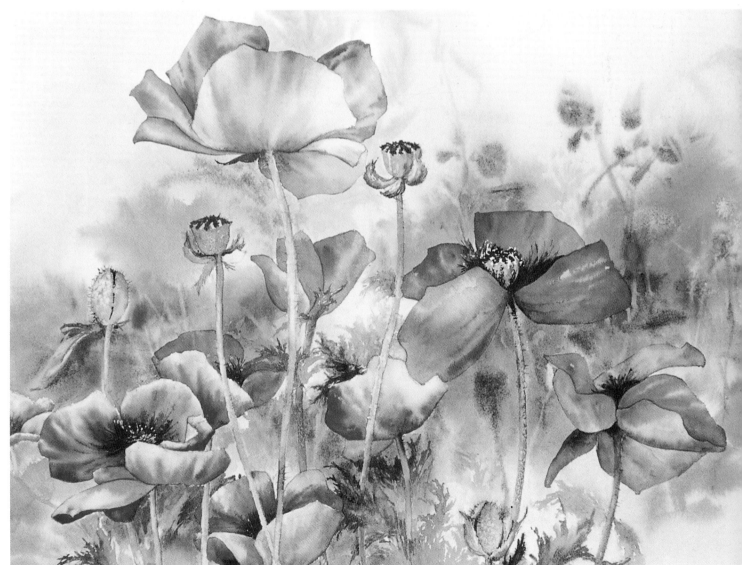

Your finished painting will have crisp edges and a loose spontaneous look in the background. **Contrast** is the key to success.

Using Japanese Masa paper...a similar approach with no preplanning

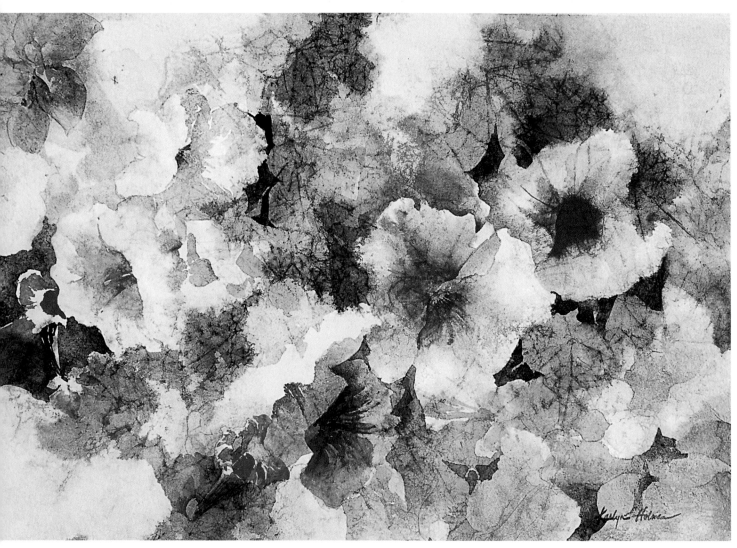

Japanese Masa paper fractures color into a beautiful network of lines similar to those in a batik. The process is all wet-into-wet and results in beautifully textured areas of softness that are perfect for floral motifs.

Masa paper has a smooth and a rough side. You should work on the rough side, so always mark that side before you wet the paper. No pre-drawing is necessary. Wet the paper and crinkle it. Carefully open the paper and place it, rough side up, on a piece of watercolor paper. Paint around the flower shapes, designing a mid-tone pattern of darks in the background.

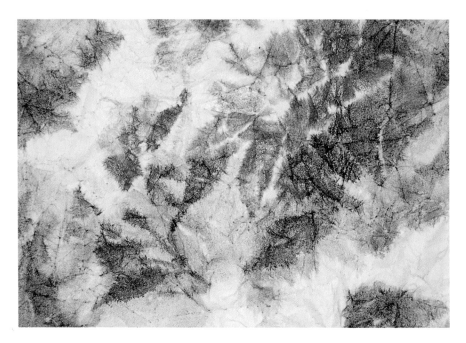

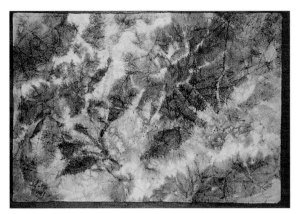

Next, paint the flowers, being sure to save areas of white.

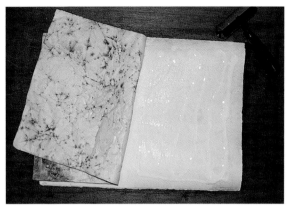

Glue half of the painting at a time onto 140# paper, using white glue diluted with an equal amount of water. Brush the glue evenly over the base paper.

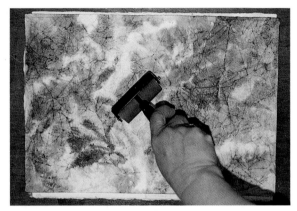

Using a roller, flatten the paper by pressing from the center of the paper to the edges, mopping up any extra glue.

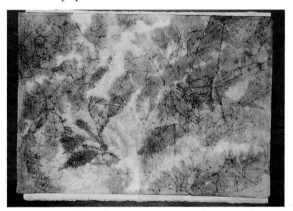

After you have flattened the paper, some of the color will soak into the base paper.

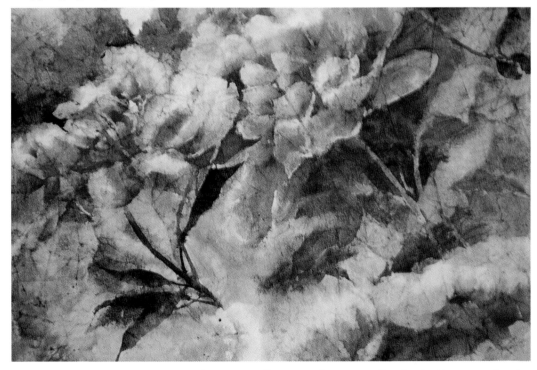

You may continue painting on the wet surface to achieve a softer look. To create hard, crisp edges, add some finishing touches after the painting dries.

Flowers first...freely splashing the background later

The integration of a soft, very abstract background and the precise interpretation of the subject gives this style of painting a "loose" look. In actuality, the process involves planning your composition for a truly successful painting. The more planning and drawing you do, the more freedom you have to interpret the background colors later.

You may choose to work with or without superimposed shapes. Using shapes adds an exciting challenge for design possibilities. I often use this style for illustrating children's books and for adding an extra layer of dimension to my paintings.

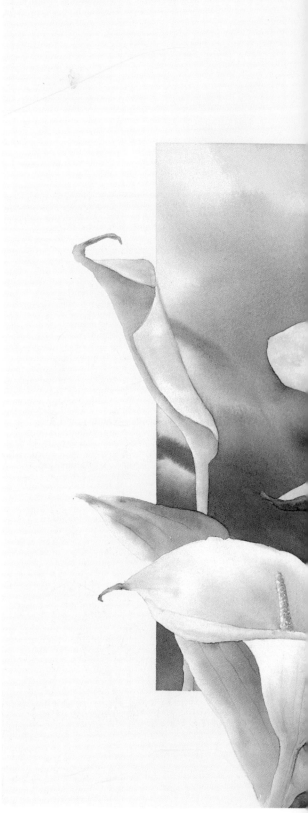

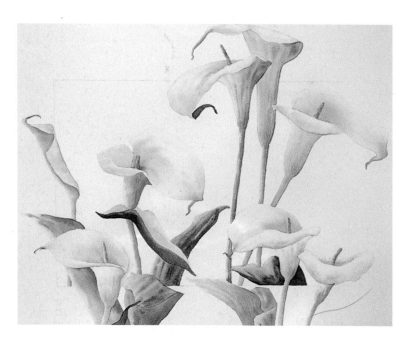

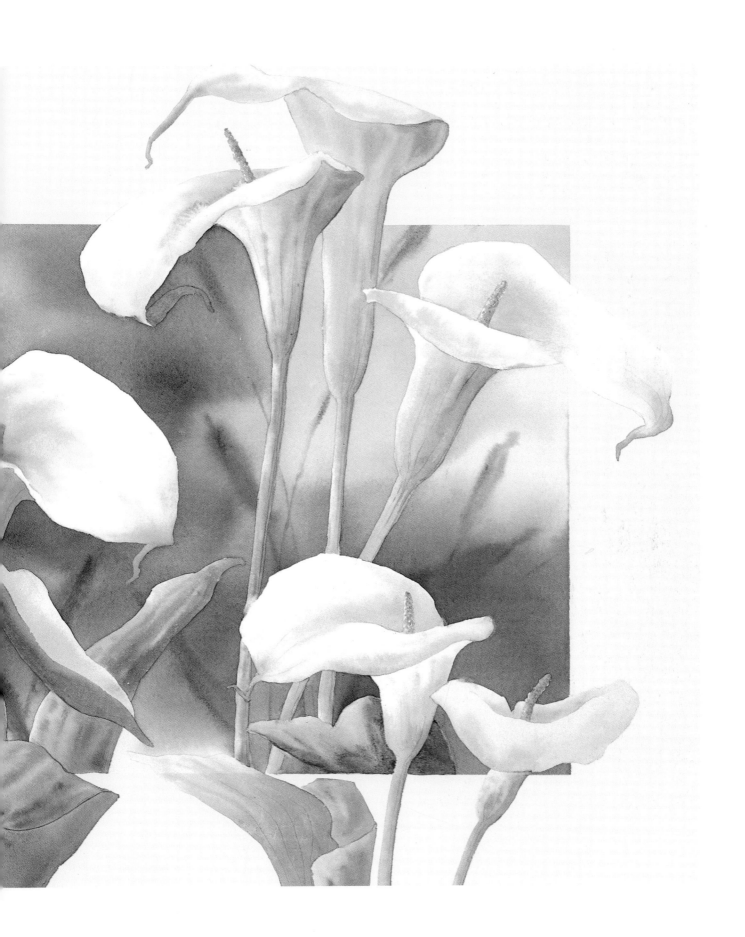

In this demonstration, the flowers are painted in a vignette style. The flowers are extended beyond the rectangular shape into the white of the paper at several strategic places. The dark and light colors that encircle the inner shape of the design become the lost and found edges. The background colors work best if they have some white or light shapes designed into them to link them with the white border.

You can take common ditch flowers and make them sparkle with freshness and show off their unique personalities. Every flower is a mini-portrait. This lesson is designed so you can complete it in several manageable steps. Use the same old "tried and true" method used for centuries— draw and plan the subject and then freely fill it in with color.

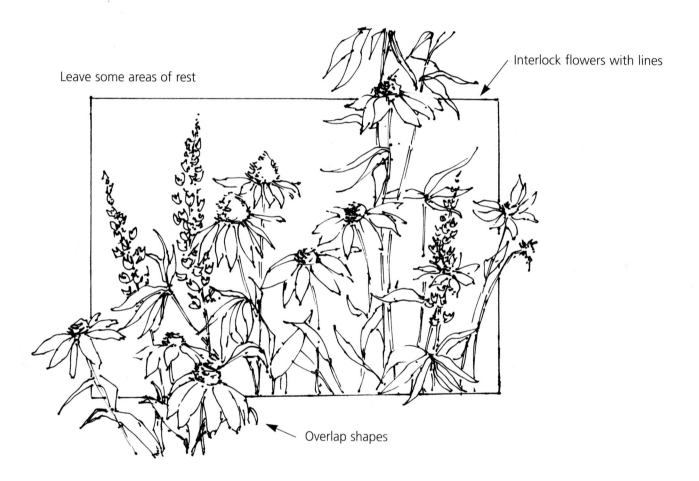

Leave some areas of rest

Interlock flowers with lines

Overlap shapes

There are four basic steps:

Step 1. Start by drawing the flowers directly on your paper. I design the linear shape after I draw the flowers because then I can decide where the line looks best. You may prefer to draw the shape first. Do whatever works for

you. However you approach the planning of the composition, be sure that some of the flower shapes overlap the borders and design as many breakouts as you desire, leaving some areas of rest.

You need to be aware of the sun side and the shadow side of each flower. Paint the center of each flower, starting with the sun side and adding harmonic colors, each a little darker, until you reach the shadow side. While the colors are still wet, paint the shadow side of the petals. Start at the outside edge of each petal and work toward the wet center. When you touch the wet center, some of the color will flow into the petal giving the illusion of reflected light. Paint the foliage with a sun and shadow side too.

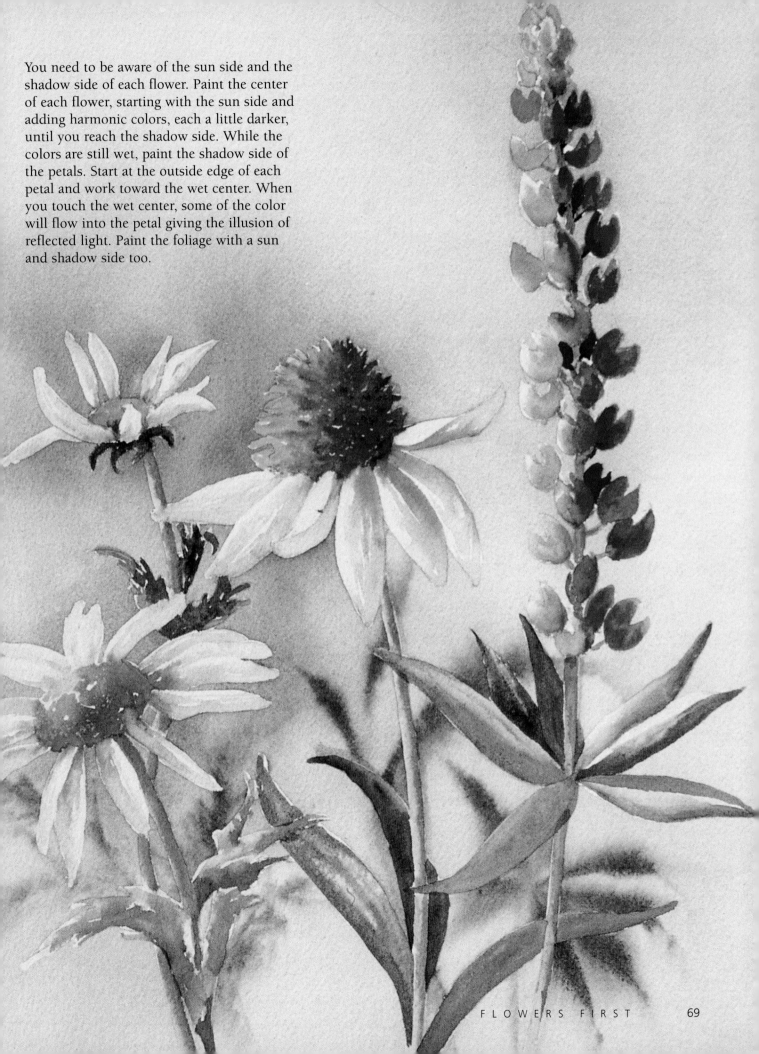

Step 2. Paint each flower as a positive shape, but do not paint any of the background. When all the flowers are painted, it is time to tape the breakout lines and mask over the flowers. **Be sure the flowers are absolutely dry.** Force dry them with a hair dryer to be sure. If the paint is not totally dry, you may lose some of the color when you remove the mask. If you have chosen to have a taped shape with breakouts, it is important to note that this area must be taped **before** you begin masking.

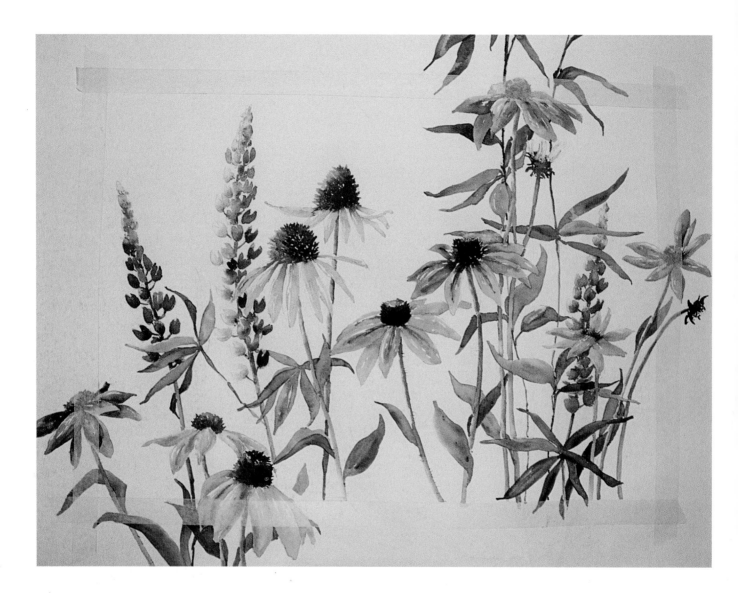

Use **clear** masking, so you are looking at the actual color of the flowers when you are painting the background. This enables you to design contrasting elements, such as light flowers against a dark background and dark flowers against a light background.

Step 3. This is the fun and free part. Paint the background with a wet-into-wet wash, creating a spontaneous and soft, out-of-focus abstract background. This lesson teaches you to view the background wash as an abstract painting in and of itself. You can use a large brush to freely flow in the color and movement.

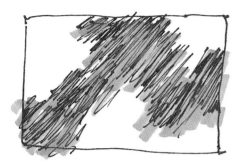

Do a thumbnail sketch of the mid-tone dark pattern. This sketch will be your roadmap for the completion of the painting.

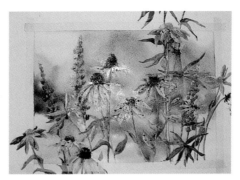

Plan your first wash to repeat the colors of your flowers and to identify the pattern of mid-tone darks.

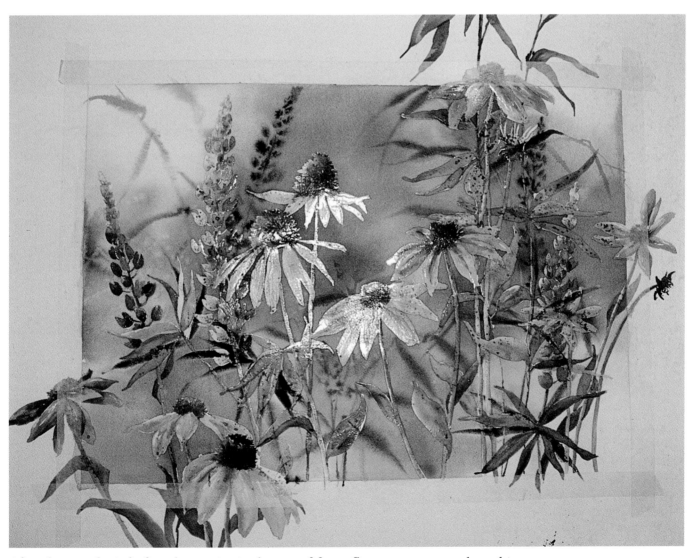

After the initial triad of washes, paint in the out-of-focus flowers, grasses and anything else you are inspired to add in the background. Remember, none of the colors you choose will mix with the colors that are protected by the mask, so you may choose any colors you like.

Step 4. After the paper is dry and before you remove the masking, add any crisp touches to finish the painting. You might consider adding some foliage interlocking with the flowers at the breakout areas and possibly some crisp, hard-edged details throughout the painting to give that final touch.

Remove the masking. I use a wet oil painter's brush to soften any edges that may have been masked outside of the actual flower shapes. I prefer to use an old brush because the bristles are worn down. The extra stiffness of an old brush will agitate the paint in the areas that need to be softened.

Some compositional guidelines:

Design the interest area in such a way that the positive and negative areas are varied and extend to the edges of your paper. Keep your darkest darks, brightest brights, and lightest lights in the **center of interest** and balance them with neutrals in the negative areas.

Remember that **restful areas are necessary**. I personally feel that these areas of openness are critical. They provide the balance for the more active areas. Paintings need visual variety. Study master oriental paintings and you will begin to appreciate the importance of visual rest areas.

Make sure some of the shapes cross over or touch the edges of the paper. You do not want the shapes to look like they are floating in space. This touching anchors the painting, adds movement and allows the viewer's eye to move in and out of the background space.

Be sure to **vary the sizes of the flowers and overlap** some of the shapes to create more interest and add a feeling of perspective. The flowers closer to the viewer should be larger and the background flowers should be smaller.

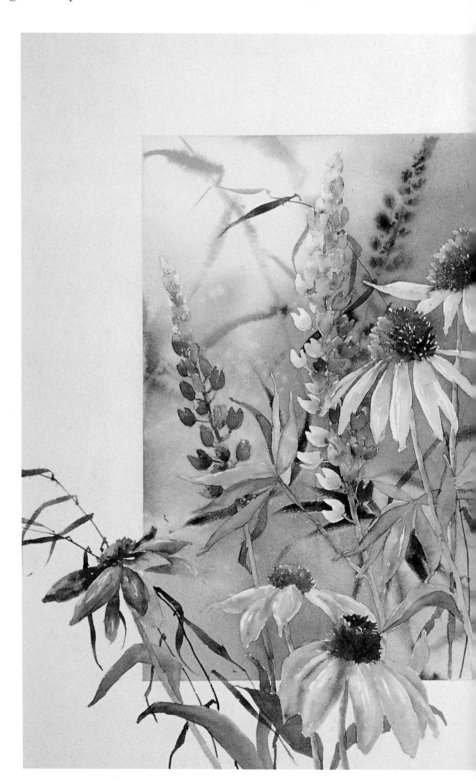

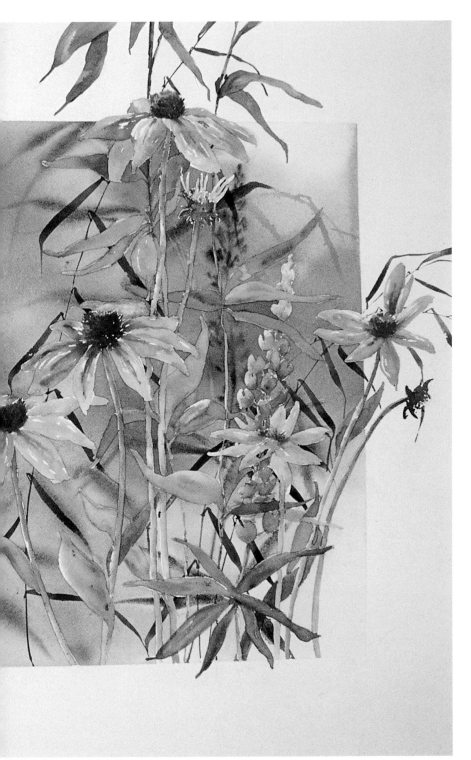

Design the **mid-tone pattern** to flow behind the entire composition. Try to create an abstract design in your background that goes beyond, yet enhances, the reality of the flowers.

Design **reversals** such as dark values behind the light flowers and light values behind the dark flowers.

Echo the colors of the flowers in the background wash.

Include a variety of **edges**. For example, soft or diffused edges allow the viewer's eye to travel easily from one area of the painting to another. Crisp edges attract attention and create drama. A blend of the two adds unity, flow and a sense of mystery to your painting.

More shape-in-shape flowers

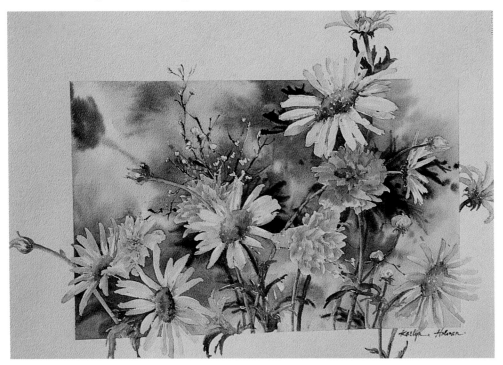

Choosing white flowers as a subject will automatically provide great contrast. In this painting, the yellow centers of the daisies enhance the yellow flowers. A hint of yellow is added into the background wash to complete the painting.

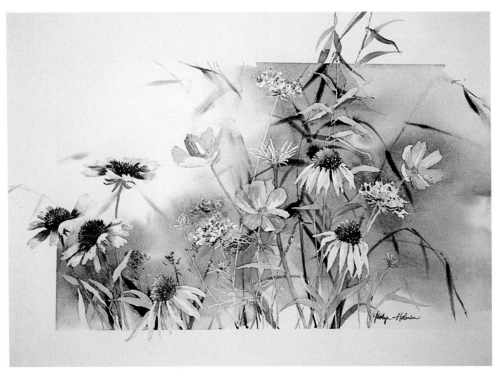

This painting of a summer bouquet demonstrates the importance of using lost and found edges. It is extremely important to design white shapes into your mid-tone background. When light shapes touch the edge, they become lost edges, allowing the white border to flow into the background lights of the painting. Also note that there are no pencil lines showing where the whites unite at the border. I purposely placed the tape near the pencil line and not directly on it. Before I painted the background, I erased the pencil line. Beware—once you have wet your pencil lines, they are very difficult to erase after they dry.

Pushing the boundaries on paintings that need a face lift

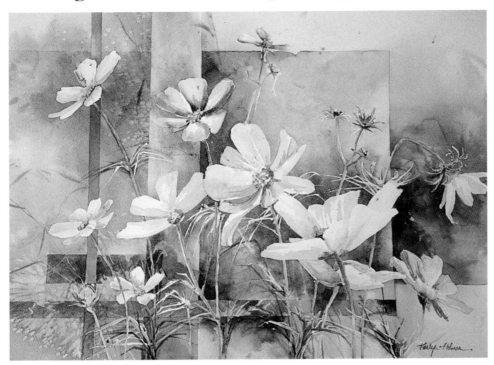

This painting needed structure and mid-tone color because the background was washed out. By designing in the shapes with pencil and painting in lost and found edges, I was able to focus on the flowers as the center of interest and add an exciting background to an "old dog" painting.

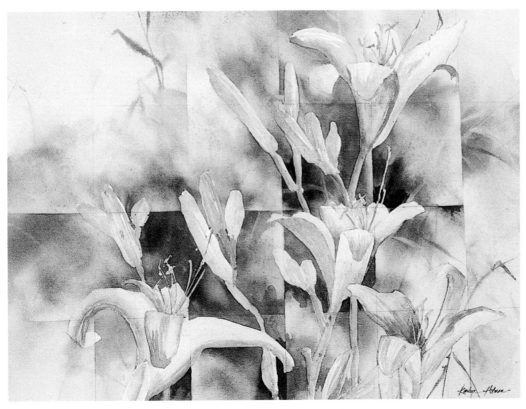

Before painting in the background, I decided to mask over the lilies. Unfortunately, I used a soft paper, so when I removed the masking, the color pulled off leaving a faded image. As usual, I looked at this surprise as an opportunity to try something new. This time I added structure using a grid pattern of equally sized rectangles. Taking a sponge and a plastic sheet, I began lifting color in checkerboard shapes and then added darks to complete the grid.

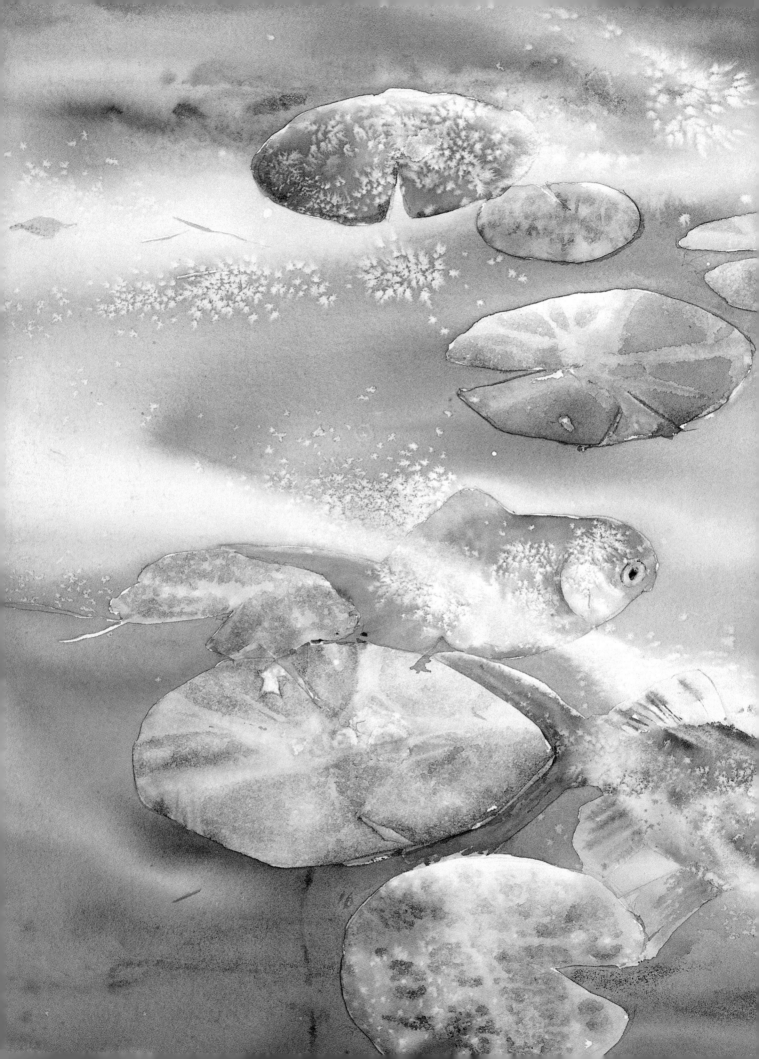

Water lilies and fish

This subject was painted using the same process—subject first, freely splash the background later. Simply draw the water lilies and fish, then paint and mask them. The fun part is painting the background wash. Wet the painting surface and apply a triad of richly mixed, primary colors. Then add more colors that will give darker values, such as antwerp blue, indigo, permanent magenta and/or whatever looks good on your subject. The really exciting part comes next. Tip the painting upright, take a coarse sprayer and spray away the color down to the white of the paper. The resulting white pattern resembles light bouncing off the surface of the water. For added sparkle, I sprinkled popcorn salt and regular salt on the painting just before the color dried.

Karlyn Holman

Balancing spontaneity with control

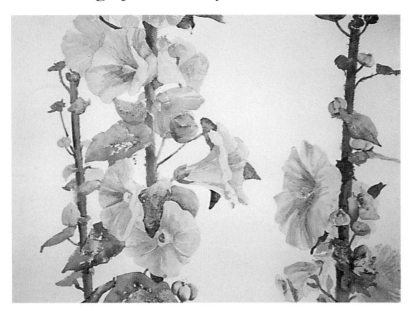

Spontaneity and control are well-balanced in this painting of hollyhocks. The flowers were painted one at a time by wetting each shape and dropping in the color. Only the positive shapes were painted and masked. The background was painted all at once, wet-into-wet.

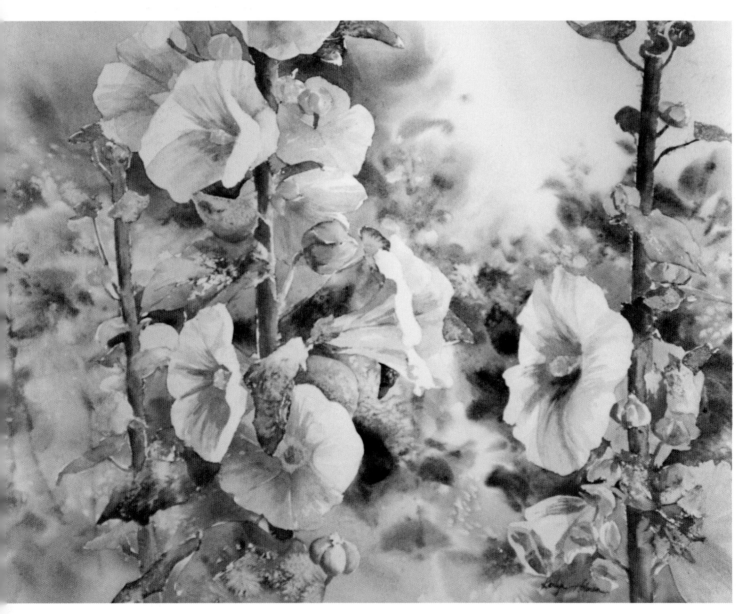

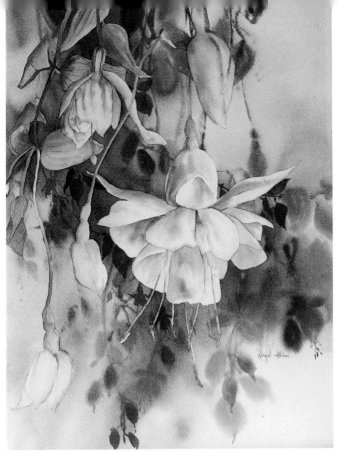

The out-of-focus background of this painting provides a dramatic backdrop for the main subject. The pale fuchsia flowers accentuate the bold colors of the foliage.

Make sure your floral images are not floating on the page. Anchor them by interlocking them with other flowers or foliage or even running the images off the page. Try to imagine that your painting extends beyond the confines of your paper.

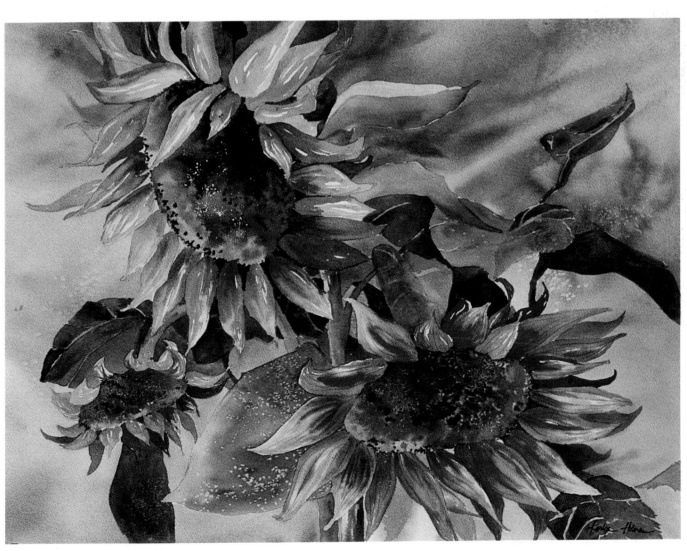

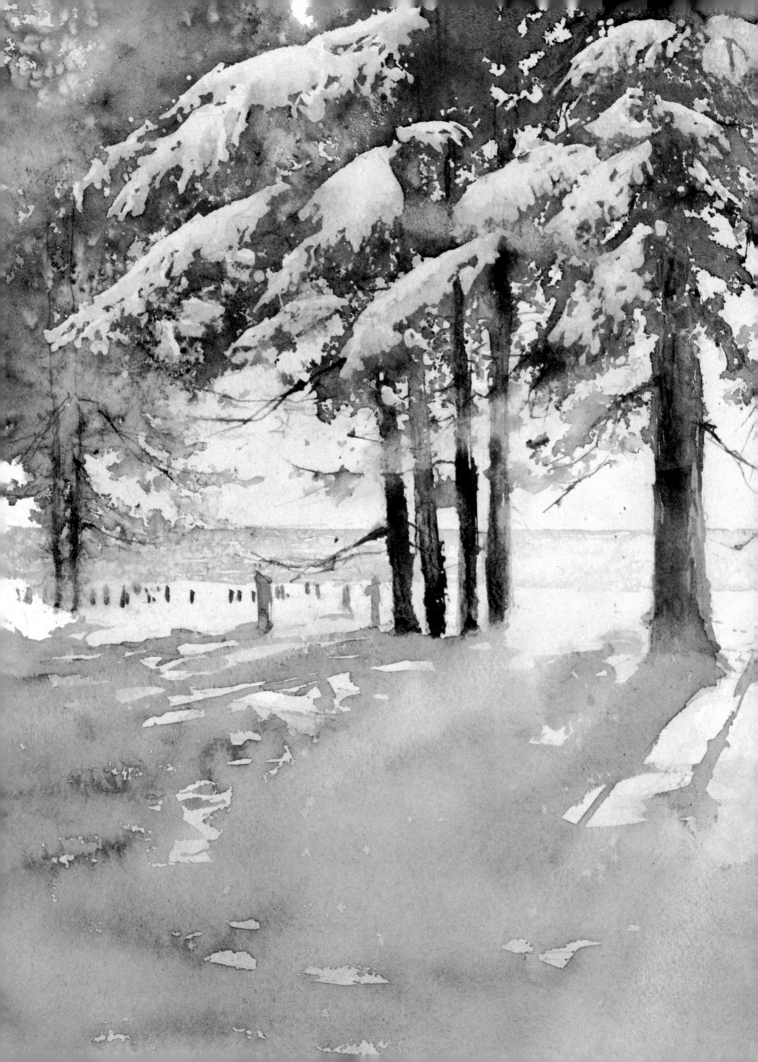

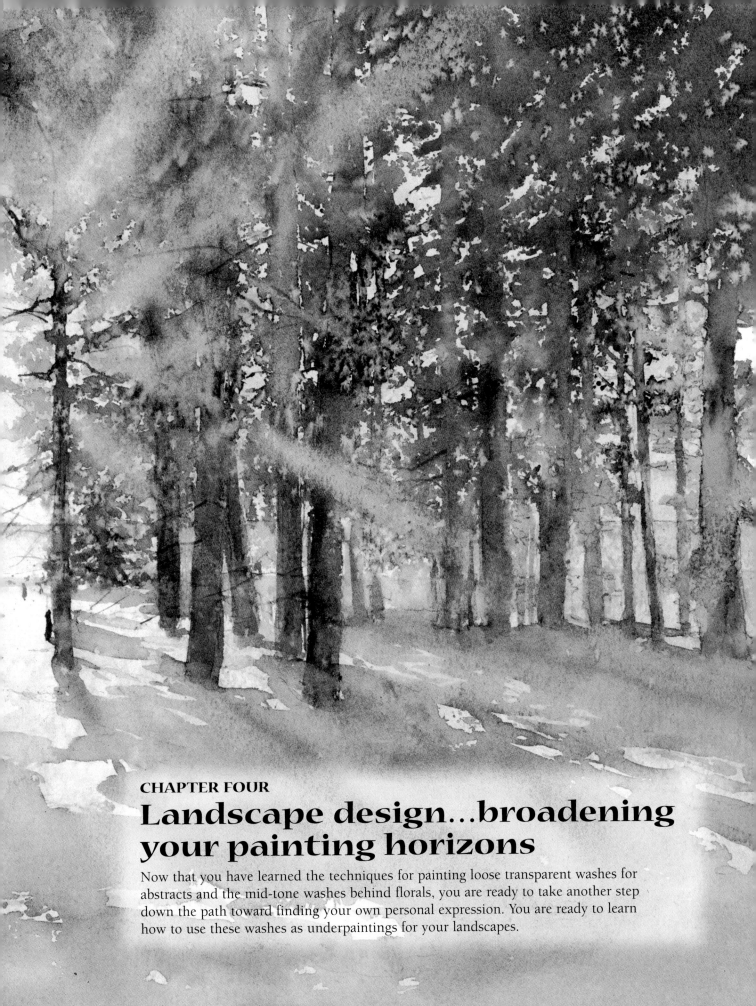

CHAPTER FOUR

Landscape design...broadening your painting horizons

Now that you have learned the techniques for painting loose transparent washes for abstracts and the mid-tone washes behind florals, you are ready to take another step down the path toward finding your own personal expression. You are ready to learn how to use these washes as underpaintings for your landscapes.

Capturing the essence...less is more

The landscape images in this lesson were inspired by my homeland. Outside my door is a lifetime of inspiration waiting to be painted. I have a sense of ownership in my relationship with the Lake Superior shoreline, the old stone quarries, and the woodlands. I experience an emotional bond with each changing season. To celebrate this sense of place, I try to capture the immediacy and expressiveness of the forms and color and stay away from unnecessary detail. I find so much personal satisfaction in just taking the color and letting it move in the water. Let the paint find the essence of what you want to express.

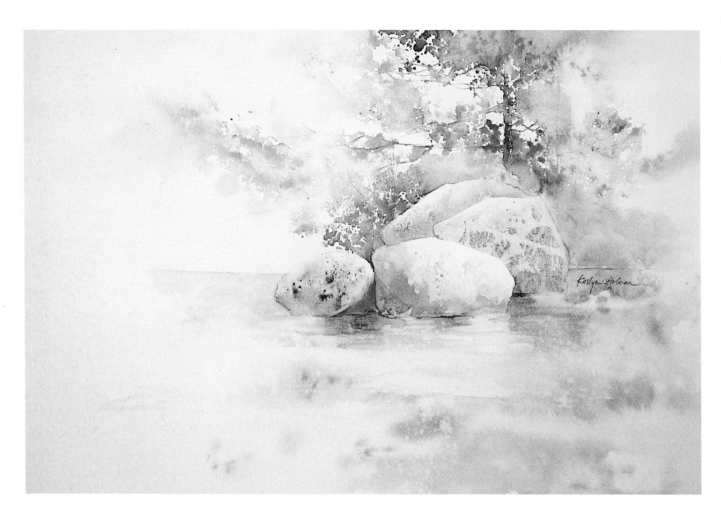

The translucent and delicate nature of watercolor lends itself perfectly to capturing the everchanging effects of the weather—misty mornings, crisp, sunny afternoons or glorious sunsets.

You will need two very important tools to do this technique. One is a **fine mister** and the other is an **oriental brush**. The fine mister is used to actually "melt" the paint into soft edges. Fine misters are available everywhere. They usually hold hair spray, deodorant, etc. You can identify a fine mister by looking at the stem inside the bottle. If the stem is very narrow, it will give you a fine mist. The oriental brush is used to drop coarse patterns of water to form the foliage. Oriental brushes are made from natural hair and release the paint much better than a man-made bristle.

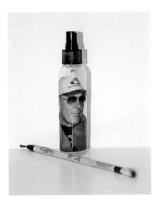

This is my fine mister and my oriental brush.

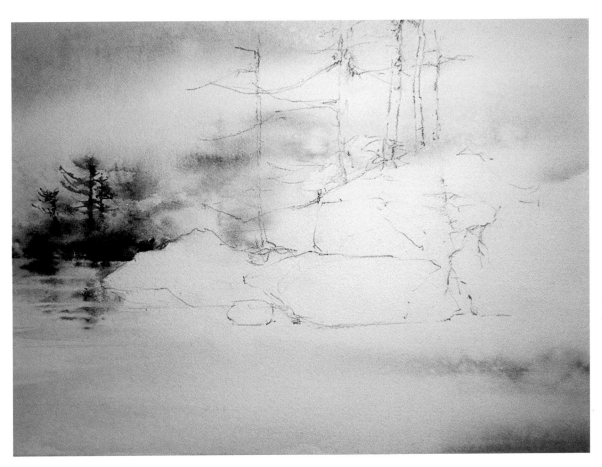

We will be working in a **vignette style**, which means that the painting is not painted with a great amount of detail to all the edges; instead, you allow some of the edges to dissolve into the white paper. To accomplish this look, you simply spray with a fine mister directly into the edges of the wet paint and watch the color move gradually into the white of the paper.

Draw a simple outline of the trees and rocks on 140# Arches cold press paper. This paper

works well because the colors will blend together without bleed-backs. Start by wetting both sides of the paper and then select a triad of primary colors. I used the triad of aureolin yellow, permanent rose and cobalt blue for this underpainting because I was trying to capture an early morning feeling. The triad you choose will determine if it is a sunny day, a dreary, wet day, or late evening. Add any out-of-focus trees by painting them in while the underpainting is still wet.

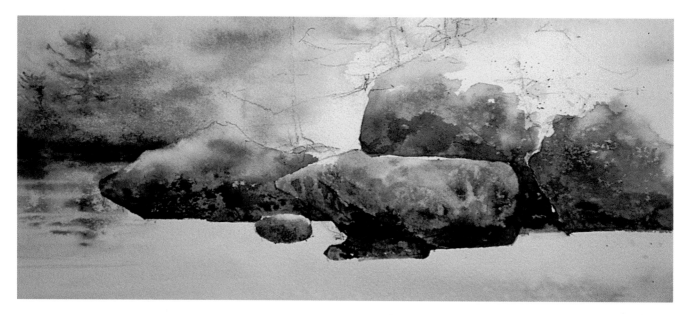

An easy and very effective way to paint rocks is by wetting each rock and dropping pure color into the shadow area, allowing the color to gradually rise up to the top of the rock. Use any warm color mixed with any cool color. By working in complements, the colors will neutralize into a rock gray when they mix on the paper.

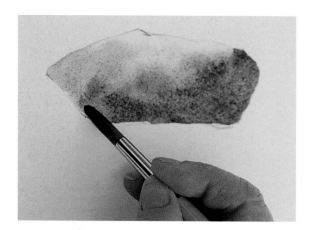

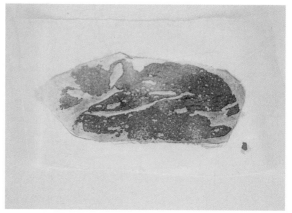

In this example, I first wet the shape and then painted quinacridone burnt orange on and layered cobalt on top of the wet orange paint. Put the color in the shadow area and allow the color to float to the top. The paint will diminish as it rises, giving the illusion that the light is reflecting off the top of the rock.

After the paint has had a few minutes to soak into the paper, place wax paper over the damp color. Leave the wax paper on until you get the desired textures you want. The longer you leave it on, the more crisp the texture.

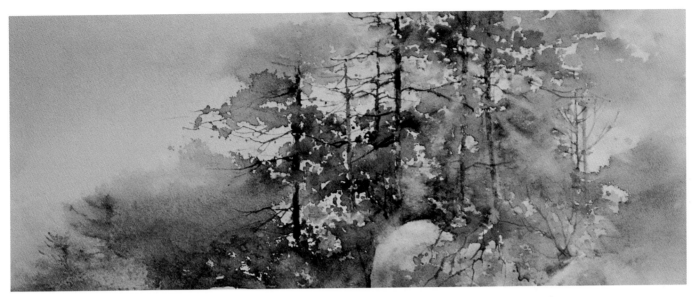

Now you are ready to create patterns of foliage to represent the trees. You should look for patterns, rather than paint each leaf. These patterns are created by dropping water from your oriental brush onto the **dry paper**. You can use a coarse sprayer if you prefer, but I find the dropping technique gives more control.

Next, you simply throw the paint into the patterns of drops, a technique I learned from Nita Engle. I love the freedom of flicking the paint using all pure colors and then letting the colors mix on the paper. The greens are a mixture of pure aureolin yellow and antwerp blue. Some quinacridone burnt orange (the complement) was thrown on top of this green to neutralize and darken the color.

All the edges are crisp at this stage, so now you should visualize where you would like some lost edges. With the help of your fine mister, you can "melt" these edges. In general, keep the edges crisp in your center of interest and concentrate on softening selected areas for contrast.

lost edges

crisp edges

lost edges

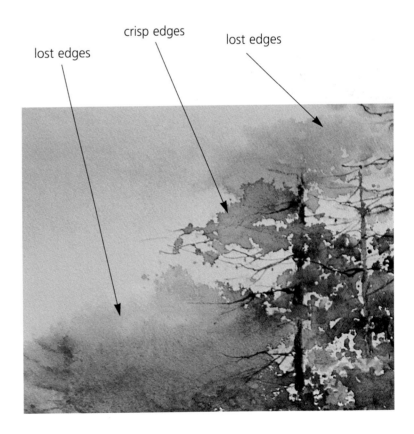

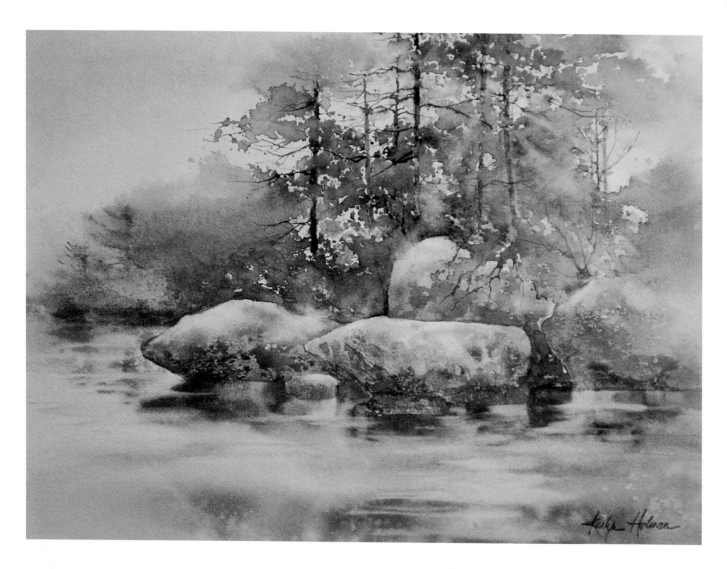

The water was painted entirely wet-into-wet. Wet only the water area, carefully going around the rocks. Reflections are distorted by the movement of the water or a breeze blowing across the top of the water, so you can invent many of the shapes. The rocks reflected in the water were painted by using the same pure warm and cool colors used to paint the actual rocks (quinacridone burnt orange with cobalt layered on top). Throw aureolin yellow and antwerp blue into the areas reflecting the trees and let these pure colors form the neutralized browns and greens. The whites were lifted out using the "thirsty brush" technique. Wet a 1/2" or 1" flat brush with clean water, then remove most of the water with a towel, leaving a dampened brush. This "thirsty brush" is like a damp sponge and literally sucks up the color from your painting. The patterns of whites created by this technique are probably the most important element in the reflections. Do not be timid—continue to lift the paint away until you can see white patterns of movement in the water. The tiny white spots were formed by sprinkling a little salt on the surface just as the paint was starting to dry.

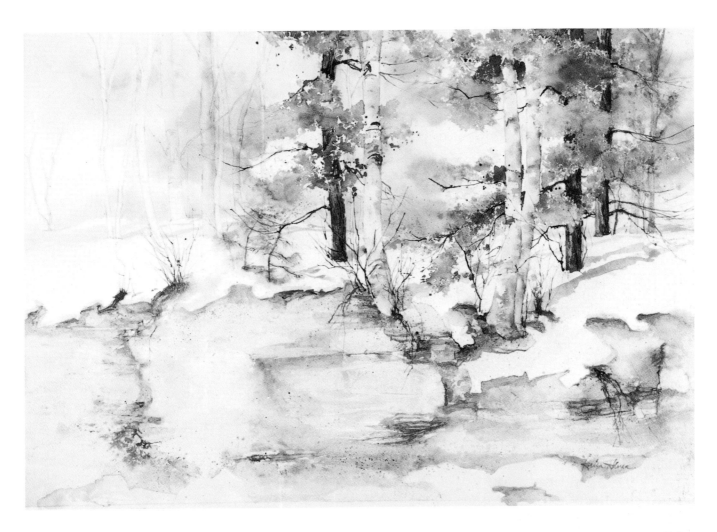

These images were inspired by an old brownstone quarry. This quarry has always been one of my favorite subjects because the colors and patterns change so dramatically with each season.

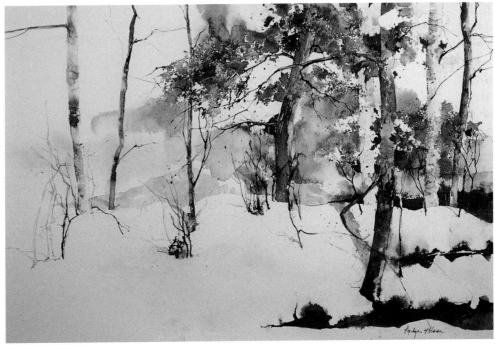

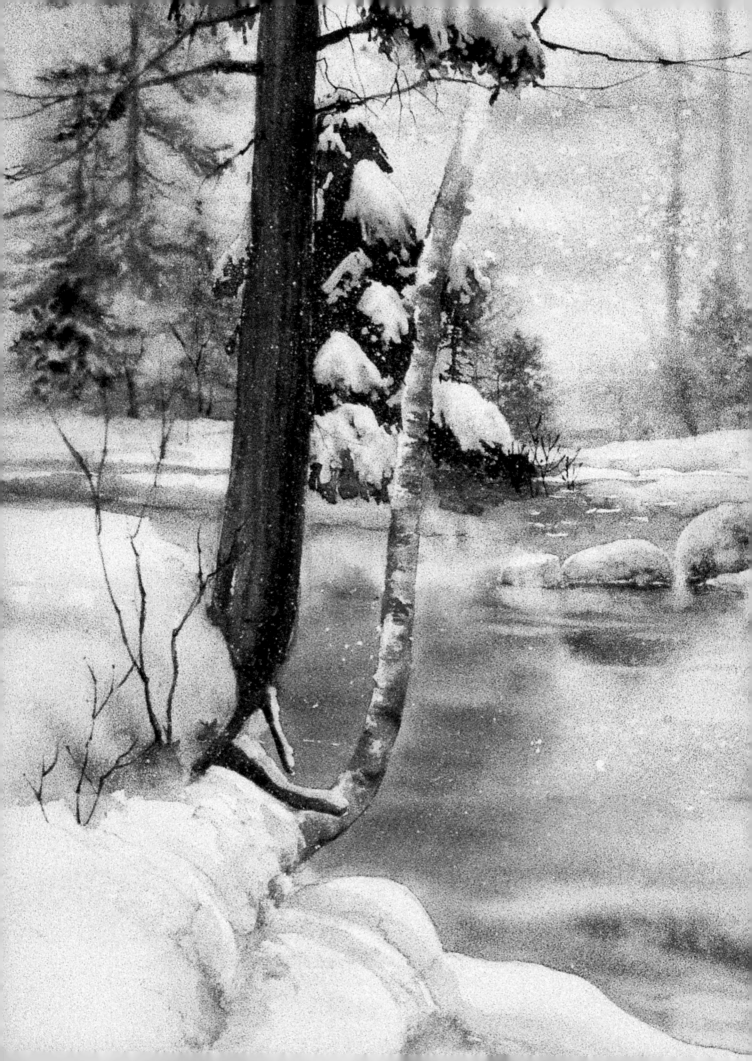

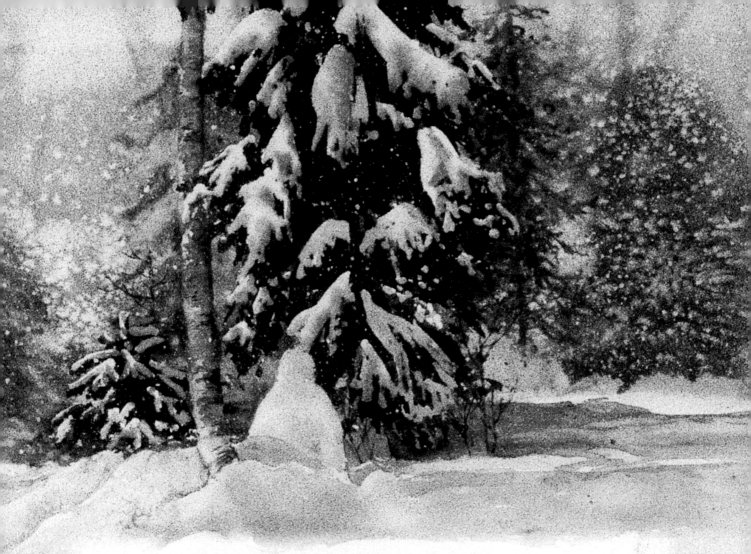

Layering color on color...a time-honored traditional approach

A winter landscape is a fascinating subject because of the large percentage of whites. These whites or lights can be designed into your painting as patterns and shapes. The whites bring out the richness of the layered color and the dynamic contrast used in other parts of the painting. This subject opens up the joy of using white shapes as a compositional tool to tie your painting together with washes of layered color. Heavy snow-laden pine branches, reflections in open river water, crisp, and sun-filled winter days are all intriguing subjects to capture in watercolor. Another compositional ploy uses the dramatic shadows created by the lower angle of the sun. This lesson involves using some masking to save the whites on the snow-laden trees. The real joy comes when you blend together the sensual washes.

This demonstration was done on 260# Winsor Newton paper because of the whiteness of the paper and the marvelous lifting potential. The colors really sing on this brighter paper. Arches would be a good choice too because this paper allows successive washes without reactivating the color. You will have to be careful with the Winsor Newton paper because it may reactivate some of the color when you layer the washes.

Step 1. Draw in the subject and mask only the snow on the trees. The snow on the ground does not need to be masked. Wet the paper only to the horizon line and lay in a triad of primary colors in the sky. I chose Winsor yellow, permanent red and cobalt blue for this painting. Tip and turn the paper so the colors will blend together. Before this wash dries, put in your out-of-focus background. If you like the effect, add a little fine popcorn salt to give an atmospheric look.

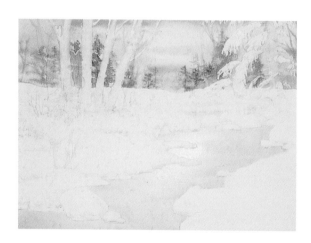

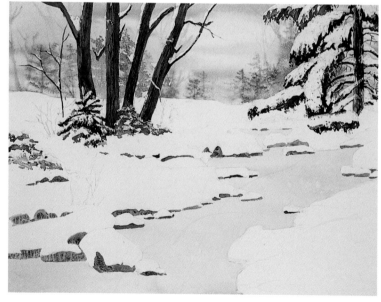

Step 2. Wet the water shape and repeat the colors of the sky in the water. You are only trying to achieve an atmospheric look because the reflecting objects, such as the trees and snowbanks, will be painted in a later wash. Lift out some white patterns and indicate some movement in the water. Tip and turn the painting as you did when you painted the sky so the colors will glow.

Step 3. Paint the dark branches under the snow-laden tree limbs. Use blue and yellow and a complement to achieve a rich, dark evergreen color. Paint any other elements you have drawn in your composition.

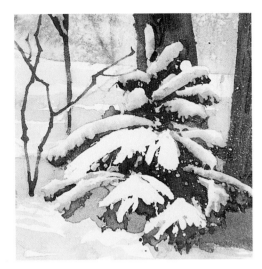

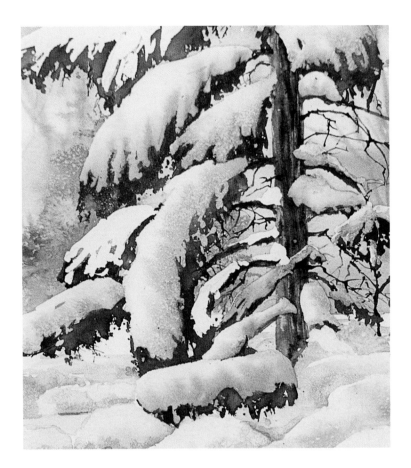

Step 4. Remove the mask and paint in the shadows on the snow-laden branches. An easy approach to capturing the light hitting the snow is to wet only the snow shape and apply a cool color, such as cobalt blue or permanent magenta, into the shadow area. Before the cool color dries, add a little evergreen color to suggest reflected light.

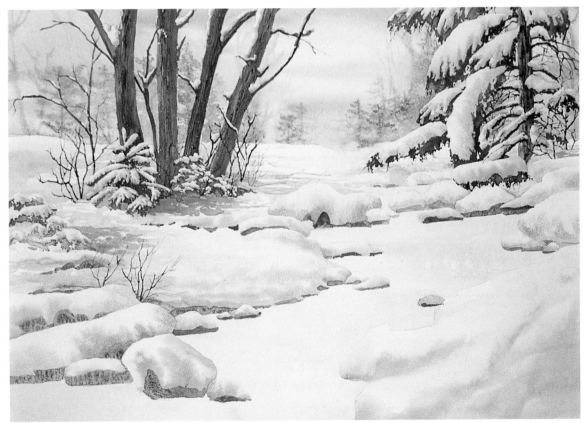

Step 5. Now it is time to paint the shadows in the snow banks. Select areas, such as the undercut banks or modulating shapes in the snow, wet these areas and add cool colors.

When the color dries, add the crisp cast shadows. These shadows will be determined by the source of the light.

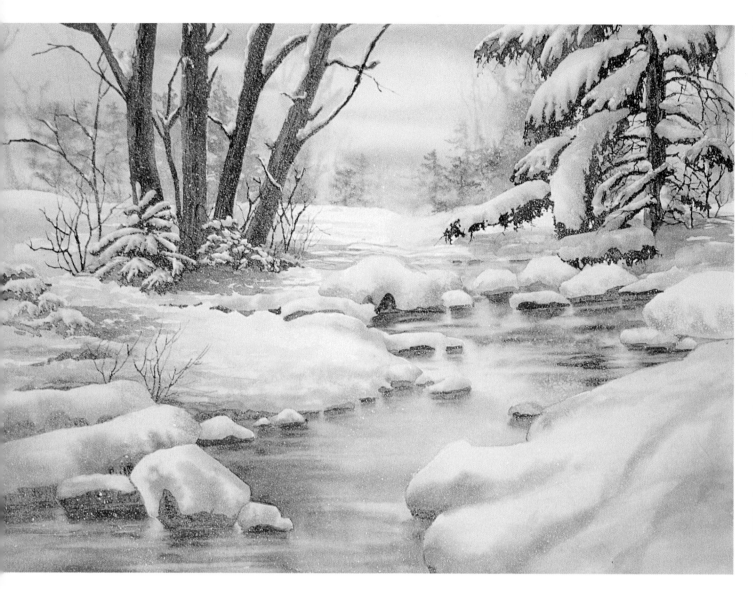

Step 6. Finish the painting by rewetting
the surface of the river and add any of the
subjects that would reflect in the water,
such as trees, snowbanks, etc. Remember,
reflections are often darker than the subject
they are reflecting. If you want to soften the
overall feeling and add a touch of romance,
you can spray acrylic white ink with a
damp toothbrush.

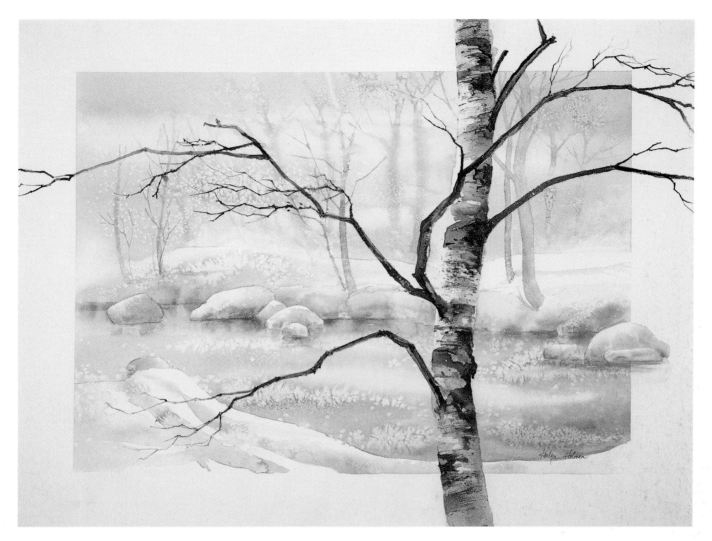

A limited palette of colors was used to create the reflections and out-of-focus background. The shape-in-shape format provided the backdrop for this portrait of a birch tree.

The pure delight of white

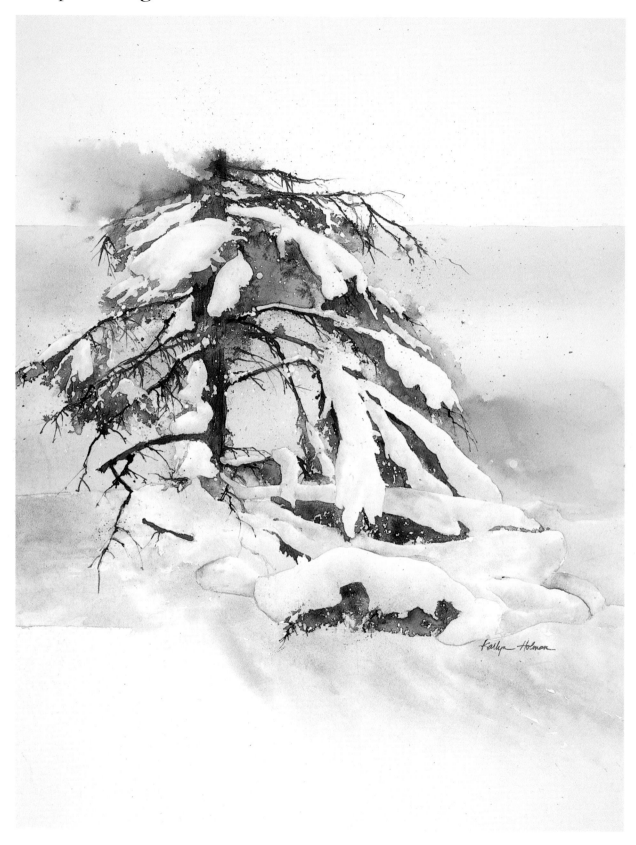

I never tire of painting my homeland in the winter. The snow abstracts the landscape into patterns, and I can push these white shapes to a bare minimum or I can interpret them with invented color. My goal when I paint winter landscapes is to find an intuitive balance somewhere between the real and the non-representational.

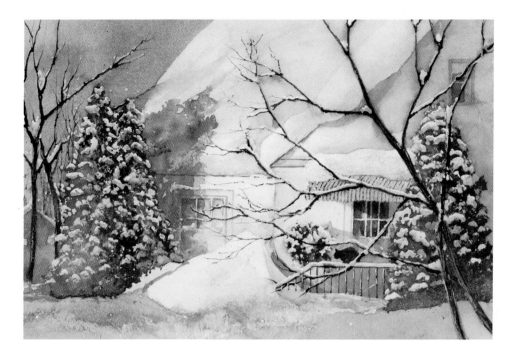

Witches brew up a ferocious storm and bury the town in my children's picture book titled *Ditch of Witches*, Bayfield Street Publishing, 1999, by Warren Nelson.

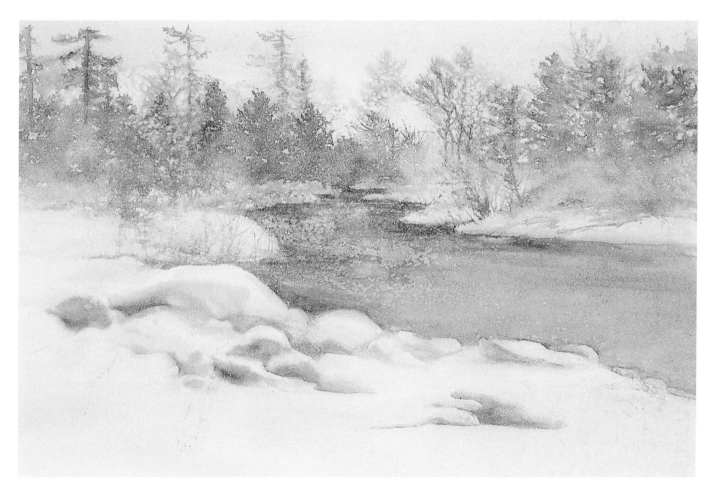

This illustration is the last page from *Christmas Song of the North*, Pfeifer-Hamilton Publications, 1998, a children's picture book by Marsha Bonicatto.

These snow scenes were inspired by photos and memories. Instead of going out on location to paint, I go out with my camera and take photographs and paint in the comfort of my studio.

Painting "en plein-air"...adventure travel

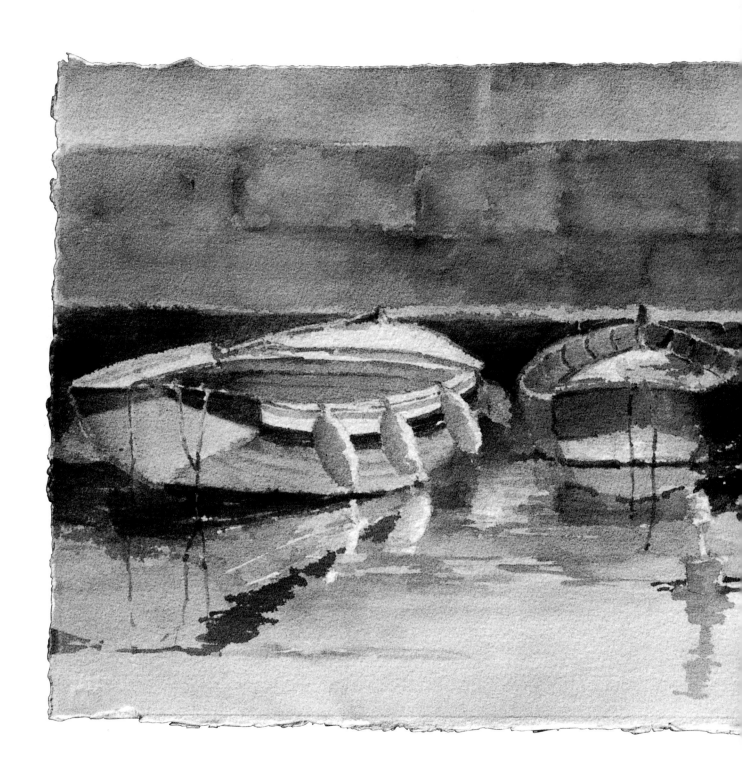

Painting on location has been the most beneficial, as well as the most challenging, experience in my journey as an artist.

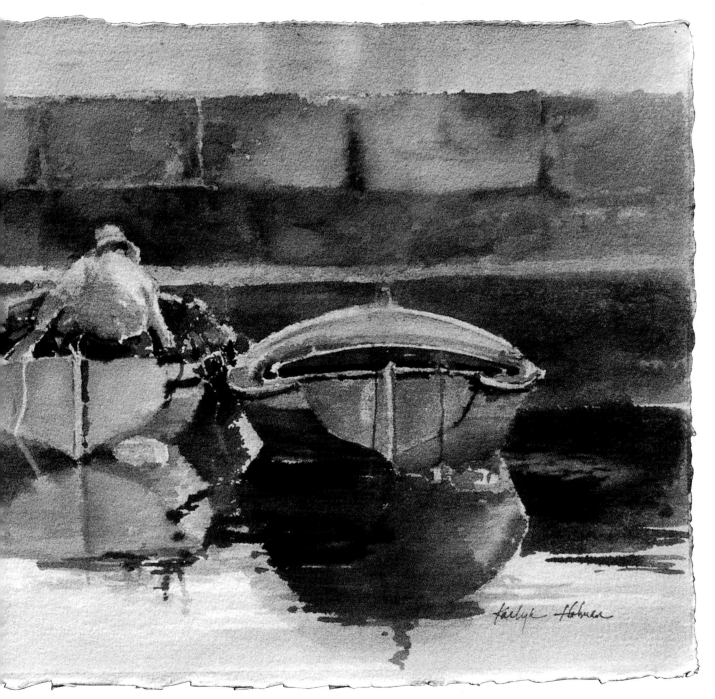

Portuguese Fishermen, 1997.

On-location painting

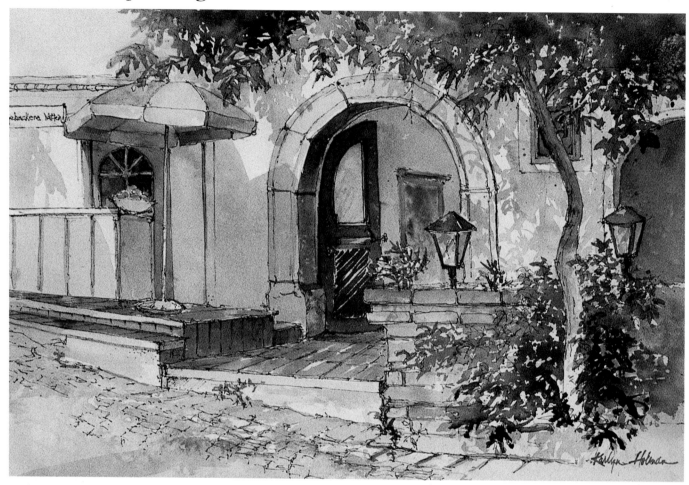

Hallstatt, Austria, 1998.

The world can be your studio and travel opens up new subjects to interpret. Every turn of the road has something to offer. When you have painted a special place "en plein-air," you will remember it forever.

One day I received a phone call from Rose Edin, a personal friend and marvelous artist, inviting me to co-host art adventures together. Although I must admit that I was not anxious to leave the comfort and convenience of painting in my own studio in order to paint on location, I knew this was an opportunity I could not pass up. We formed a business partnership and co-taught fourteen trips to twelve countries.

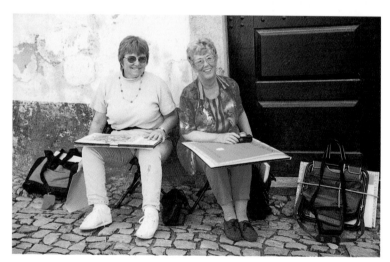

Karlyn and Rose, 1997.

When I first thought about painting on location, I imagined that I would have to carry all my equipment from place to place and hope that I would find something inspiring to paint. The reality was quite different—I found inspiration all around me. All I needed was a few brushes, paper and a palette of colors.

The locations we traveled to had subject matter everywhere…my major problem was deciding *what* to paint. The inspiration I have received from painting "en plein-air" can not be measured and has been the most positive influence on my growth as an artist.
Thank you Rose!

Why paint on location?

The immediacy and the inspiration of being right there cannot be compared to trying to paint from a photograph. When you are actually on the scene, the subtleties of color, changing light, smells and energy draw you into the experience. Painting on location has been the most beneficial, as well as the most challenging, experience in my journey as an artist. I have always felt that on-location painting requires a more direct style and that my wet-into-wet style would not be appropriate, but I have since changed my mind. How you paint, directly or otherwise, is not important. *What* inspires you to paint is what matters!

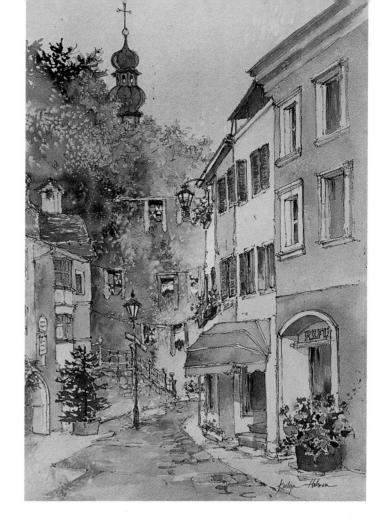

Brunico, Italy, 1998.

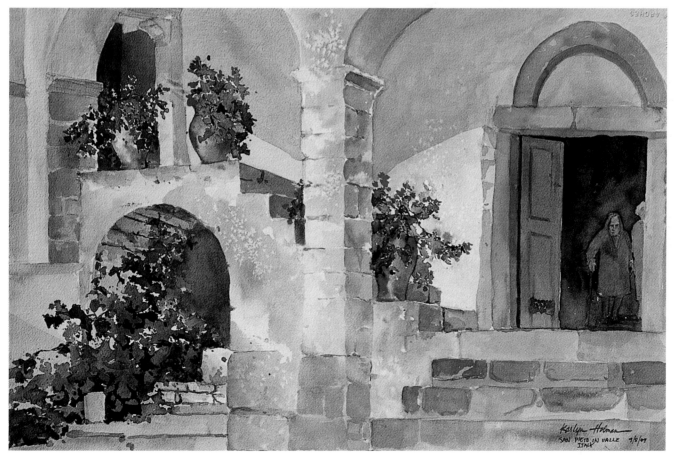

San Pietro in Valle, Italy, 1999.

What to bring

All artists have their own on-location para-phernalia that they prefer. Some like easels; some sit directly on the ground. I like a light-weight stool. These three- or four-legged stools only weigh a pound and a quarter, so I take two along, one to sit on and one to use as a table. By keeping my equipment to a bare minimum, I can spend more time moving around searching out the subject.

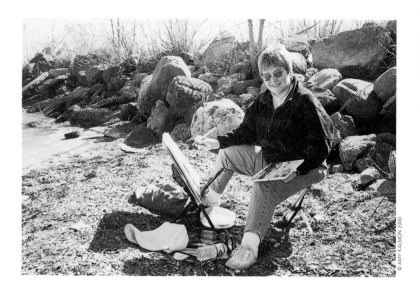

I take the following items on location:

Lightweight umbrella for sun and rain
Small palette filled with paint
My favorite brushes in a holder
Pencil and eraser
Water in a screwtop bottle (for drinking and
     painting)
Container to hold painting water
Tissues or toweling
Sharpie® ultra fine point permanent marker
     by Sanford®
Staedtler Lumocolor permanent #313 pen
Maskoid and soap in a reclosable plastic bag
Sketchbook
Assortment of half-sheet papers
Fine mister bottle
Coarse sprayer bottle
Portfolio made from foamboard
Four bulldog clips
Lightweight bag with shoulder straps
Salt (film canister works well as a container)

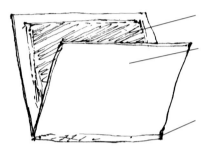

15" by 22" paper

Two 1/8" foamboard pieces cut slightly larger than the paper

Tape the two pieces together so they can fold shut and open easily

When you are looking for a place to paint, consider avoiding the bustling crowds. In noisy, congested areas, I photograph subjects for later consideration. To avoid painting in the direct sun, try to anticipate the movement of the sun over the course of the day. You may set up in the shade only to find yourself in the direct sun shortly thereafter. Wearing a hat (or a napkin) helps to cut the glare.

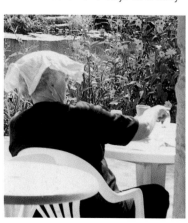

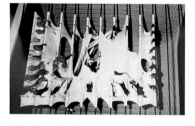
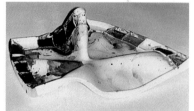

Obviously, these artists did not listen to my "recipe" carefully!

I advise artists to fill their paint wells and allow them to dry thoroughly before leaving on a painting trip. Often, artists in distress call me at the last minute because they forgot to fill their paint wells. I used to say, "Hey, no problem! Just fill your wells and put the palette in the oven at 200°F, turn off the oven and open the door." After seeing a few well-done palettes, I now simply advise using a hair dryer.

100

These photos show the infinite variety of ways artists work on location.

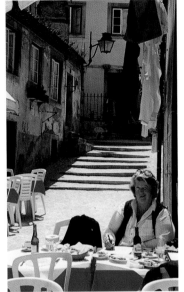

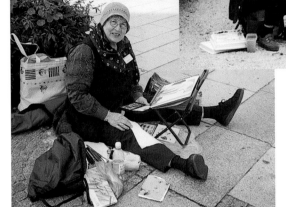

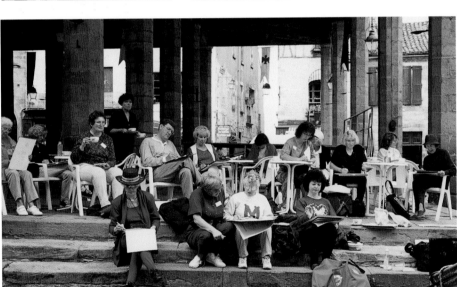

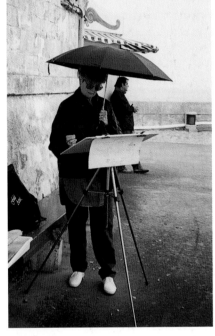

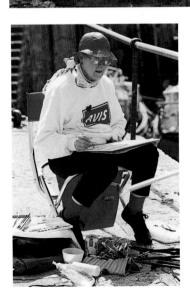

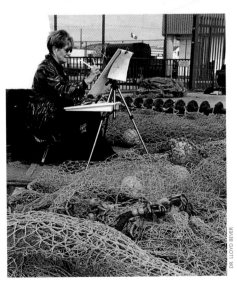

DR. LLOYD BEYER

Choosing a subject

Finding a subject to paint is always part of the adventure. I have painted the "picture post-card" areas and the "out-of-the-way" places. I have painted close-ups and panoramic views. All are fabulous! As an artist, you must carefully observe the selection of subjects before you settle in on the shapes and patterns of light that excite you. Many factors influence the outcome of your painting. Should you chose a vertical or a horizontal format? Intimate or panoramic view? Warm or cool mood? Some of your efforts may not be successful, but every effort will be a learning experience. On-location painting is a time to explore and grow and gain confidence.

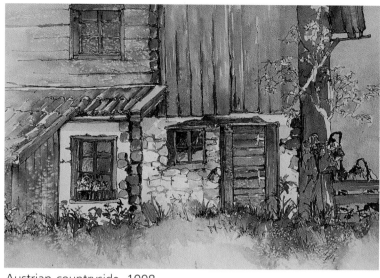

Austrian countryside, 1998.

Selecting a close up view of your subject takes away the need to worry about converging lines of perspective. Because you are focusing on an intimate scene, your composition becomes an abstracted arrangement of vertical and horizontal shapes, giving your realistic painting an abstracted design. This is a great way for first-time "en plein-air" painters to approach their subject—move in close, design dark and light patterns, balance detail with areas of rest, play with textures, invent diagonal light patterns to balance the strong horizontal and vertical patterns and just enjoy the detail.

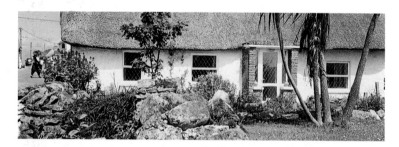

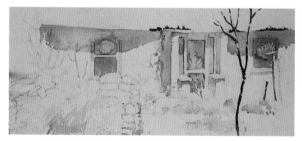

Seaside cottage in Ireland, 1999.

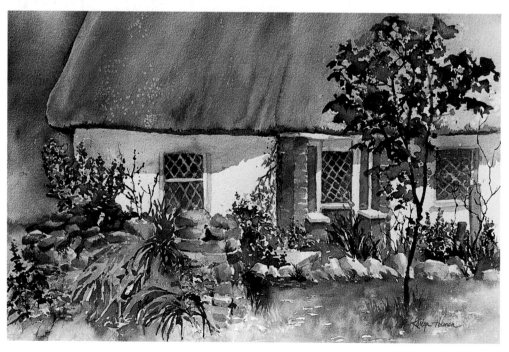

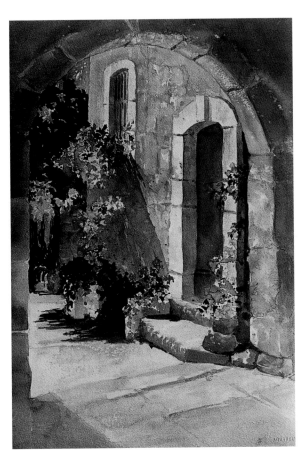

After you have learned to observe your subject straight on, you can expand your viewpoint to include converging lines of perspective.

Umbrian hill town,
Italy, 1998.

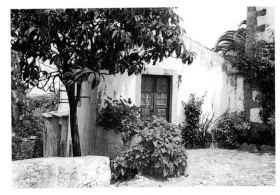

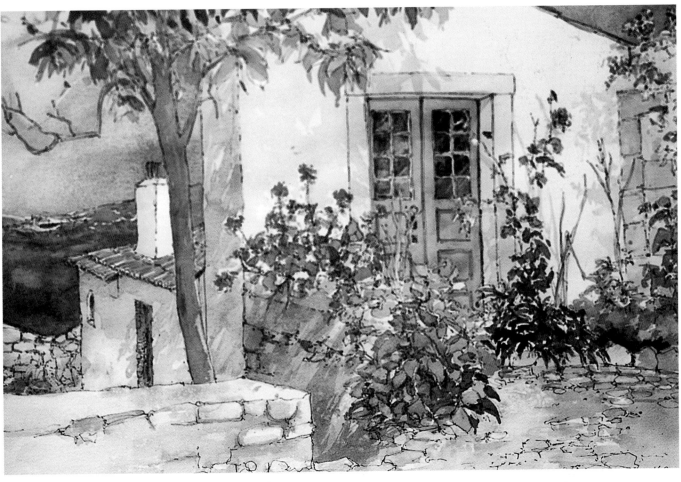

Obidos, Portugal, 1997.

Expanding your horizons

You may not always be able to be on location at the ideal times of mid-morning or late afternoon when the shadows are most interesting. Try to make the best of the moment. If it is raining, try to capture the foggy, diffused atmospheric look. If it is sunny, try for crisp edges. If there is no sun, concentrate on the flatness of the subject. Every situation has its own challenges—**flexibility** is the key word to enjoying the experience.

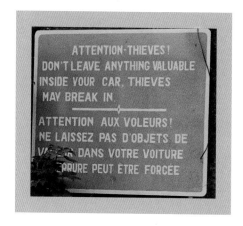

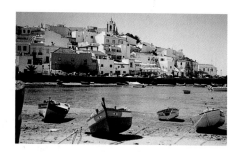

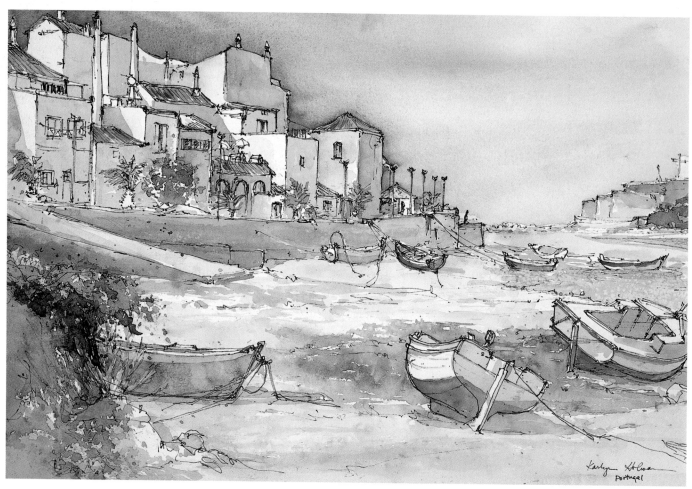

Algarve, Portugal, 1997.

After you have gained more experience, expand your horizons to a more panoramic view. This small fishing village in the Algarve in Portugal, 1997, was a treasure trove of painting subjects, from the boats at low tide in the foreground to the buildings in the distance. When I drew the boats in this painting, the tide was out, but when I actually did the painting, the tide was in. Painting on location is always a challenge and a great way to stretch your creative talents.

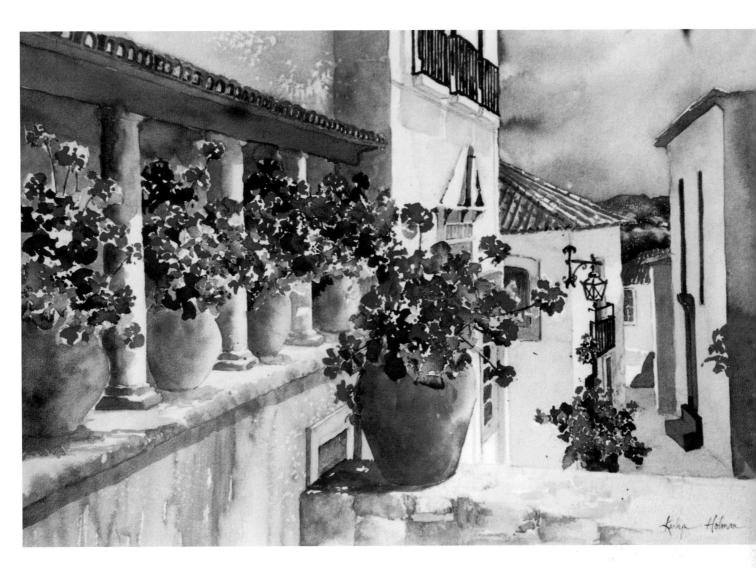

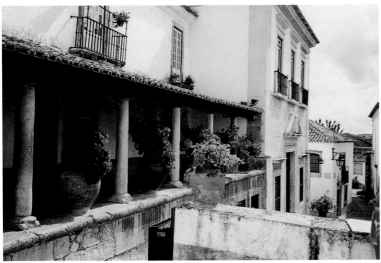

The village of Obidos, Portugal, 1997, had so many inviting subjects—narrow street scenes, colorful flowers against the white-washed buildings, wrought iron railings, the beautiful vistas all around—we could have stayed and painted for weeks.

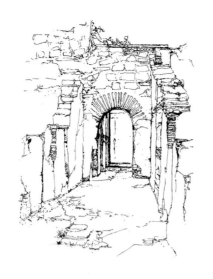

Be flexible—follow your heart

On my first visit to Guatemala, we painted the traditional ruins and colorful flowers and found the fountains and historical sites very appealing. On my second trip to Guatemala, I was once again looking forward to capturing the colorful Guatemalan landscape when suddenly, the rhythm of the trip changed, and we became infatuated with the Mayan people.

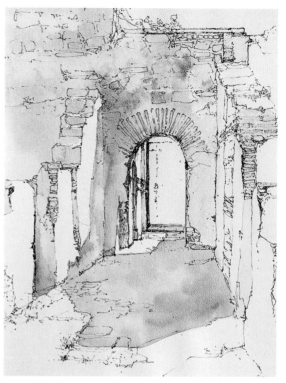

Antigua, Guatemala, 1994.

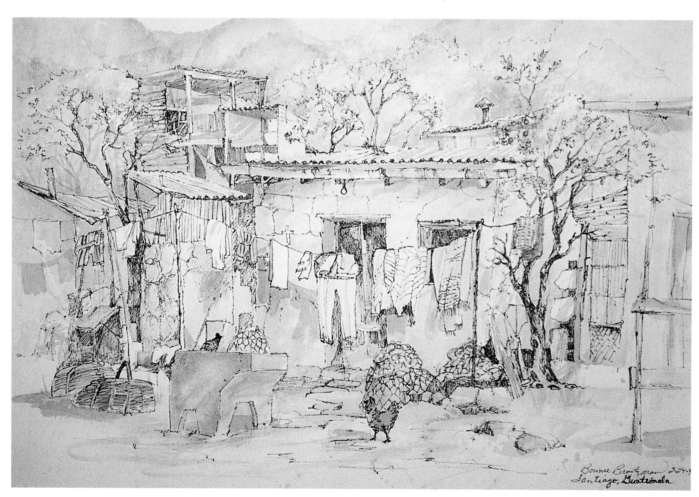

This painting by Bonnie Broitzman, Santiago, Guatemala, 1996, is an example of how unique, cultural experiences can suddenly become available to an artist. Bonnie purchased a hammock from an artisan and he invited her to paint in his courtyard. She met his family and was privileged to paint an exceptional subject.

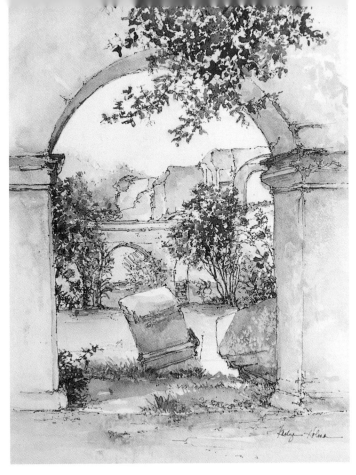

The convents, monasteries and most historical sites are in ruins because of several earthquakes. The roofs are caved in, creating unique patterns of light and dark subjects.

Antigua,
Guatemala, 1994.

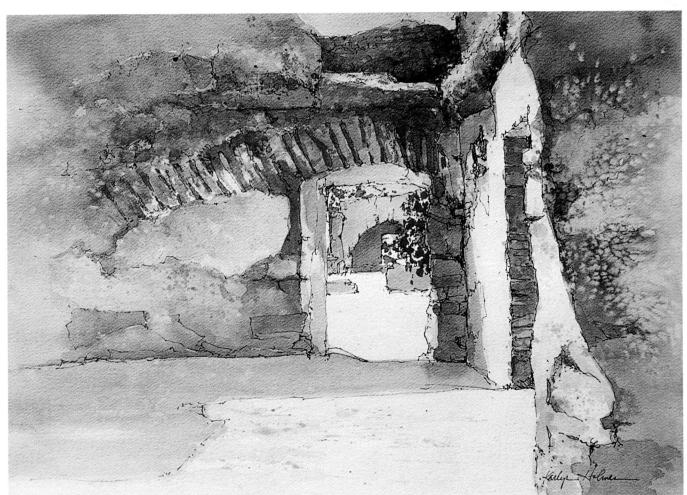

Antigua, Guatemala, 1994.

Getting to know the Mayan people

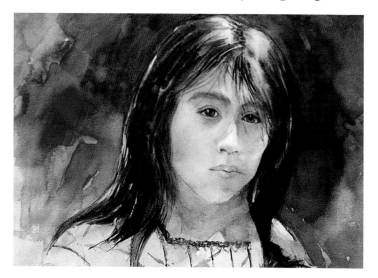

Even though we had little experience with portraiture, the faces of these children suddenly became our focus. The Mayan children were incredible subjects, willing to hold a pose without wiggling. We visited schools and playgrounds and small villages and always found willing subjects to pose for us. On this particular trip, we had enough time to be flexible and follow our hearts. I value my drawings from this experience as much as my finished paintings.

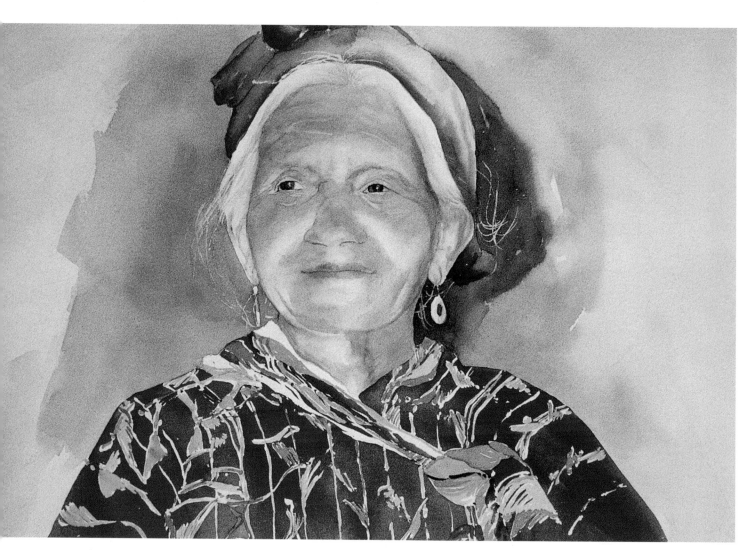

This Guatemalan lady joined us for coffee and sold us her wares. She was a fascinating subject with a thousand stories in her face alone. Language was no barrier.

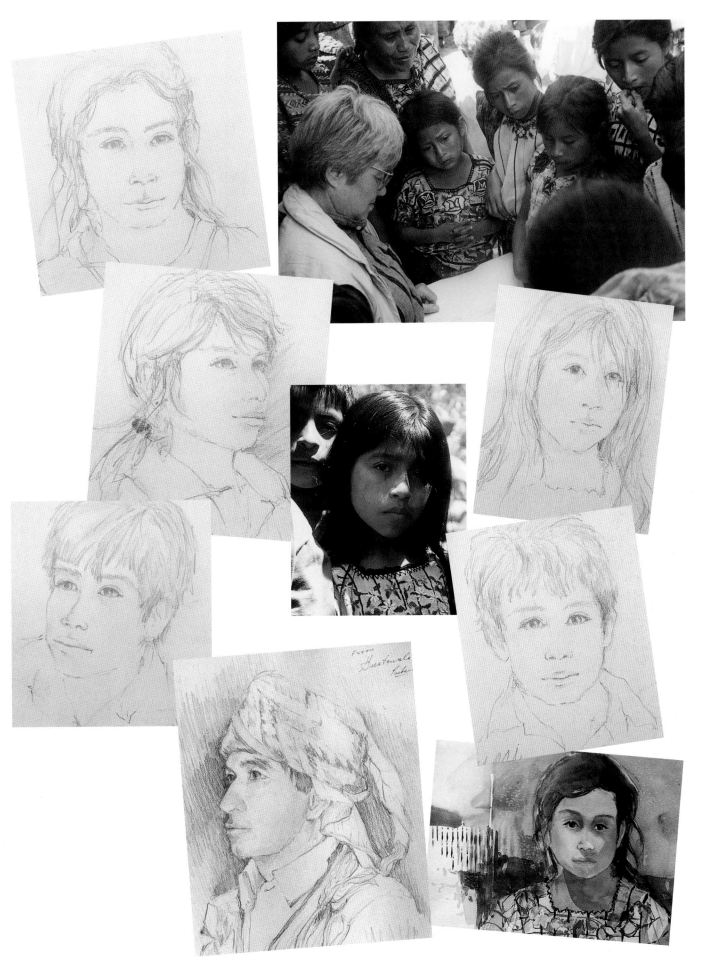

To edit or not to edit? That is the question.

I am a realist at heart and usually find myself focusing on detail. Painting on location has taken away some of the easy control I usually experience in my studio and has made me learn to respond quickly to changing light and limited time. Painting what you can capture in a photograph will always be a temptation, but when you paint on location, you have to quickly decide what will make a good composition. Exercise your "artistic liberty" and draw only what interests you. Just say "no" to things that do not add interest to your composition and train your eye to focus on the important elements.

On our trip to China in 1996, I had reached my "pagoda quota" and was ready to explore a new subject. While some of the workshop participants were painting an exquisite pagoda on one side of the bridge, I glanced to the other side and quickly sketched this intimate view of a private home, leaving out some of the unnecessary detail and focusing only on the elements that interested me.

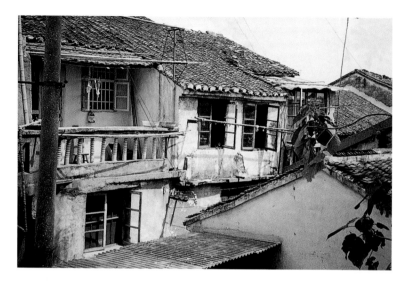

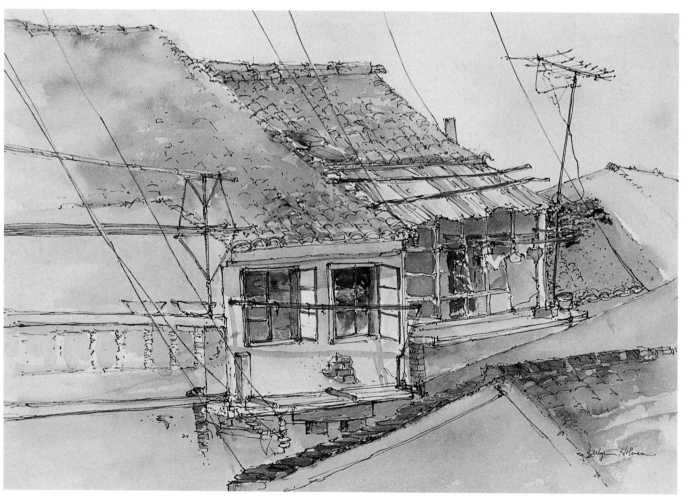

When I painted this scene in Portofino, Italy, 1990, I was overwhelmed by the variety of subject choices. Shakespearean players in full costume were wandering the street, a sailboat regatta filled the harbor and the townspeople were going about their everyday business against a beautiful old-world backdrop. After letting my senses roam, I finally zeroed in on the old-world buildings and boats.

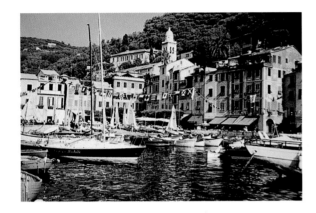

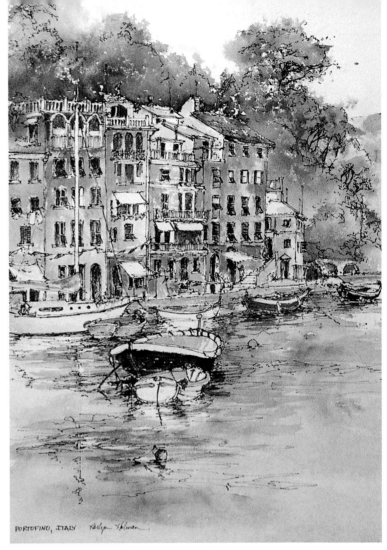

This busy port in Rethymnon, Crete, 1994, was a challenging scene. Again, I was completely overwhelmed by the number of boats in the harbor, the numerous sidewalk cafes full of people and the beautiful old buildings. I wanted my painting to express all these elements, but I realized that I had to edit out unnecessary detail. I purposely selected two boats, a few buildings and the suggestion of an outdoor cafe to tell the story.

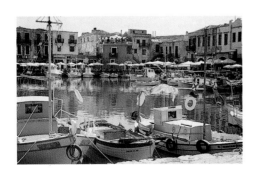

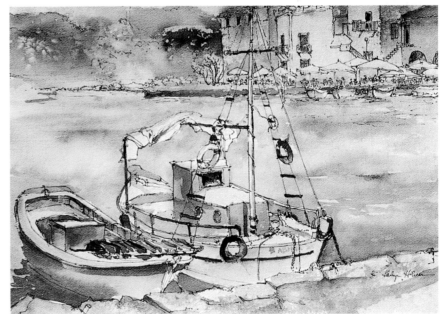

Perspective

There are two types of perspective, linear and aerial. They are both easy concepts to learn and essential to a good painting. If you take the time to learn and apply the rules of perspective to your painting, you will gain immense confidence as an artist.

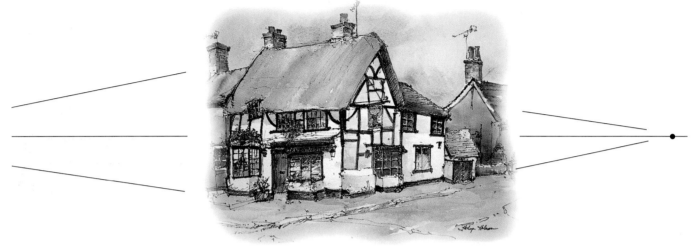

All parallel lines eventually converge in the distance and end at one or more vanishing points on the horizon. This point is often located beyond the boundaries of your painting.

Linear perspective creates the illusion of three dimensions on a two-dimensional surface. Perspective relies on rules that are easy to learn. In my experience over the years, I have found that the basic premise to understand is that **your eye level and the horizon line are the same thing**. Once you know where the sky meets the earth or where your eye level would project to meet the subject, the rest is easy. Simply project your eyes onto the scene in front of you. Everything at eye level is a horizontal line. Everything below your eye level goes up to the horizon line, and everything above your eye level goes down to the horizon line. You can be tricked if you just look at the subject, so it really helps to visualize this imaginary line to guide you. Once you learn the rules and learn to look for these lines of perspective, drawing becomes a piece of cake.

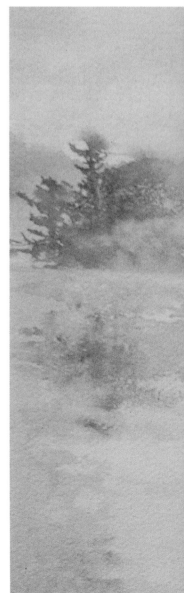

This painting was painted early one morning just as the sun was breaking through the mist on a mountain lake in Hallstatt, Austria, 1998. The light was diffused, the edges of the mountains appeared and disappeared, and all the values were nothing more than subtle variations of gray. This was an extraordinary opportunity to paint entirely wet-into-wet and try to capture the delicate tonal variations. Try this atmospheric style of painting yourself. Simply select a triad of primary colors and let the colors blend and neutralize on the wet surface. I used cobalt blue, permanent rose and aureolin yellow for my initial wash because as they blended on the paper, they became more muted and dissolved into an atmospheric landscape. Painting mist and fog is a great exercise in working with complements. Create a haunting image by working with softened and blurred edges.

Atmospheric or aerial perspective is simply interpreting the air between you and the distance, with colors softening and appearing more blue as they recede. Cameras often put everything in focus, but painters can choose to paint this atmospheric tempering and add a sense of mystery to their paintings. Atmospheric perspective is accomplished by controlling the intensity of your lights and darks and colors. By using complementary colors and neutralizing these colors into grays, you can create this atmospheric look.

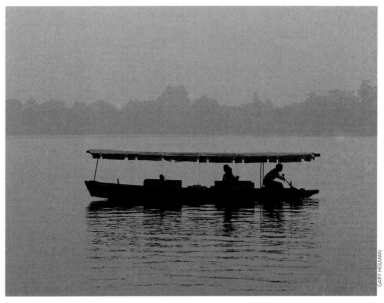

Suzhou, China, 1996.

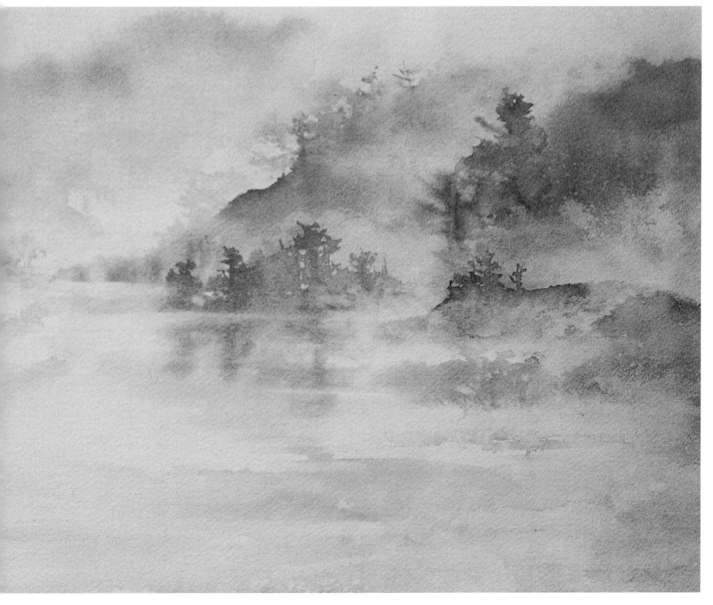

Values…the roadmap to a successful painting

Values lead your eye through a painting, like a roadmap leads you to a destination. Every painting has a range of values, from light to dark; however, not all paintings need a full range of darks and lights. You may choose a high key or low key approach. The emotional quality you are trying to capture will suggest what type of values you may want in your painting.

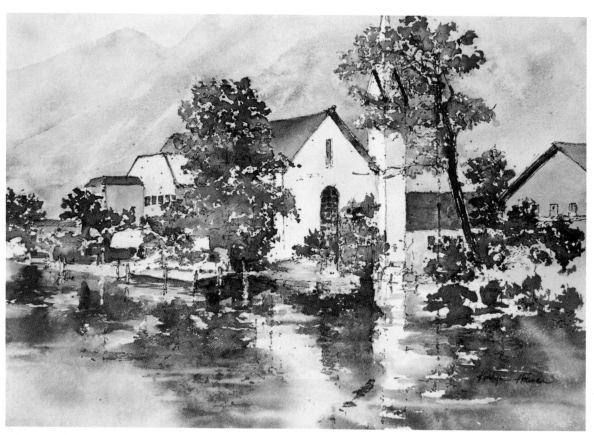

This painting of Hallstatt, Austria, is an example of strong light and dark values. This painting has a story to tell. Our trip to Austria was almost cancelled because of an airline strike, but we were ultimately able to secure a flight schedule that included a nine-hour layover in the Chicago airport. This layover provided an opportunity to teach and paint together and this demonstration painting was completed in the airport.

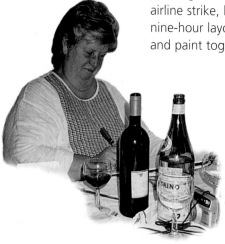

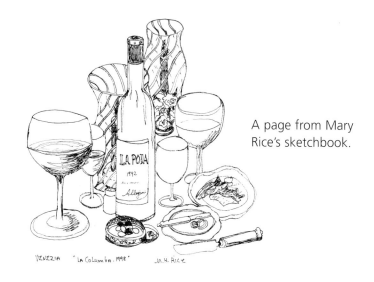

A page from Mary Rice's sketchbook.

Carry a sketchbook at all times. It will help you use your time in an inspired way whenever you have the opportunity.

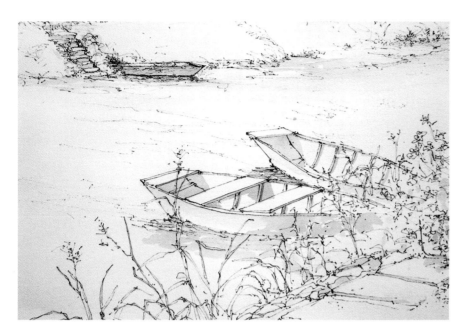

This painting of flat-bottom boats in France could easily have ended up looking like two paintings, the river bank on the top and the boats on the bottom. By interweaving a vertical grouping of dark values, I was able to tie these two elements together.

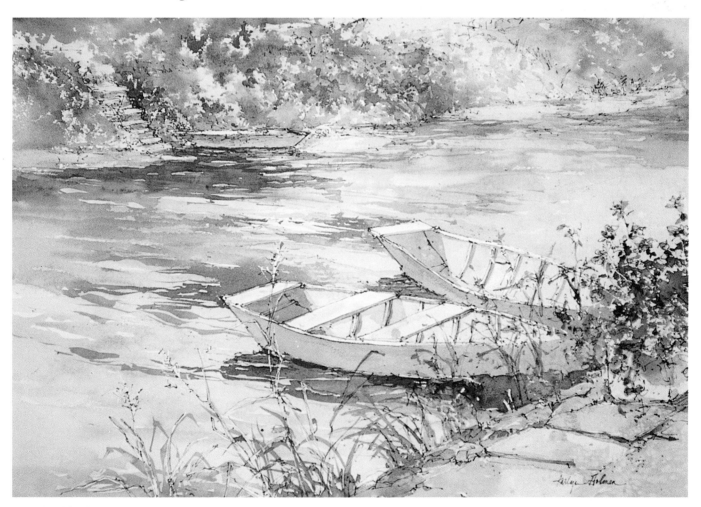

Marais Poitevin, France, 1995.

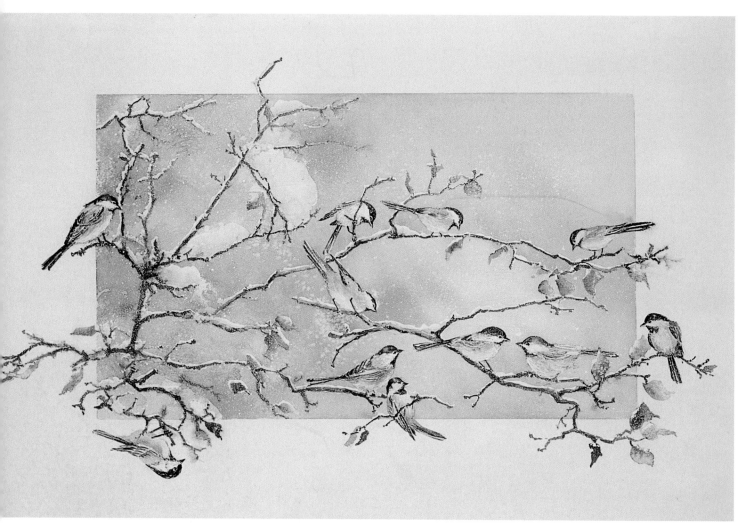

This **high key** painting of eleven chickadees has almost no darks. My intent was to create a light, joyful feeling by concentrating on warm colors. The painting is from one of my children's picture books titled *Christmas Song of the North*, Pfeifer-Hamilton Publications, 1998, by Marsha Bonicatto.

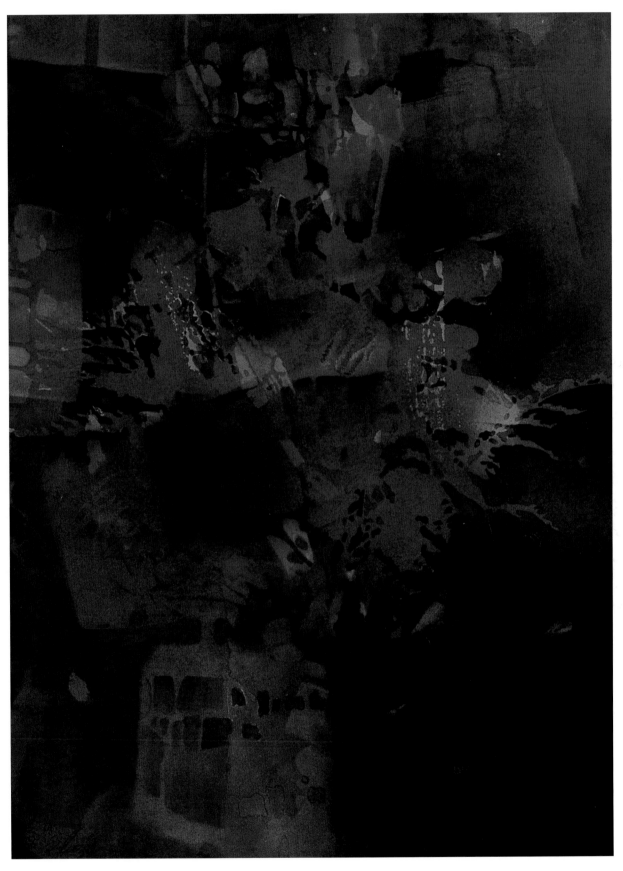

This **low key** painting by Susan Luzier has very few lights and evokes a moody feeling. As Susan explained, "In FLOWERS BY JERALD, I worked with the interlocking and overlapping of both wet-into-wet and glazed shapes. My goal was a dark and mysterious painting surface. Maskoid was used to retain the light areas. The subject was the silhouette shape of a dozen roses from my sweetheart."

Compositional Guidelines

The design elements below have been formulized by every teacher far and wide; follow these "tried and true" rules to help you with your composition.

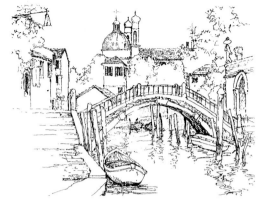

Design your **focal area** slightly off center.

Add **texture** in selected areas. I suggested texture by selectively painting some of the steps and random ripples in the water.

Invite the viewer to **enter** the foreground of your painting by using a strong directional movement. By making the canal wall converge into the painting, I am able to lead the viewer into the center of interest. A foreground lined up in a strict horizontal movement can be boring. Any diagonal movement created by using elements such as steps, cobbled streets or rows of flowers draws the viewer into the painting. Invite the viewer to experience what you experienced.

Use a variety of **size relationships**.

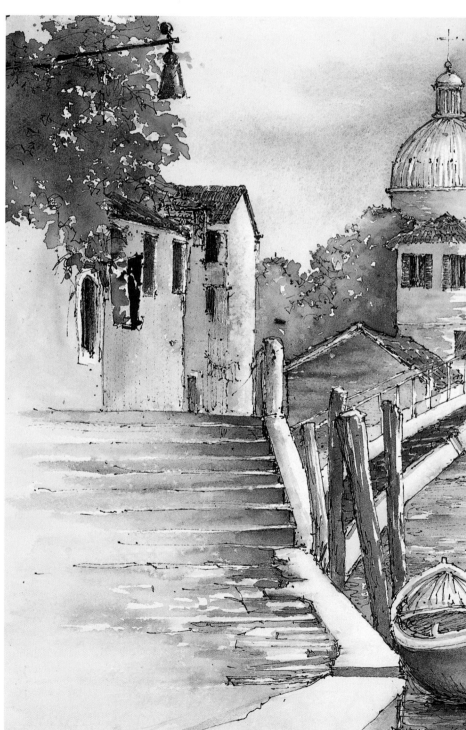

Drawn on location in Venice, Italy, 1991.

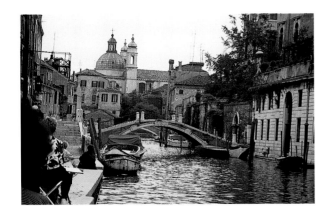

If you follow your own intuition and draw on all your past experiences, your painting will take on a personal interpretation.

Edit out unnecessary elements by simplifying the background to enhance the center of interest.

Use **overlapping and interlocking** shapes to hold the composition together and gain perspective and depth.

Design in **value** and **contrast**, such as an atmospheric background and in-focus foreground, dark colors next to light colors, warms next to cools, crisp edges next to lost edges, and large shapes next to small shapes. Keep searching for ways to add contrast.

Repeat colors throughout the painting to add **color unity**.

My allegiance to realism always wants to take over when I am in front of a subject. I want the perspective to be correct and the shapes and scale to be as close as possible to the real thing. It has taken me years of on-location painting to finally convince myself to edit out unimportant detail and not be a slave to realism.

On location…a cultural as well as educational experience

My favorite "out-of-the-way" place is at LaRomita. LaRomita, a 16th-century Capuchin monastery in the Umbrian hills of Italy, is now an International School of Art. Every other year, I share this facility with artist friends, and we paint every day in the nearby hill towns. When you take the time to stay in one place and absorb the silence and the sounds, the smells of dinner cooking, the fragrance of flowers and the graciousness of the villagers who invite you into their homes to share coffee and sometimes their home-made wine, you experience a more intimate level of observation. Painting on location is definitely a cultural, as well as educational experience. The camaraderie experienced by artists traveling together creates opportunities to try new approaches and techniques. Painting all by yourself can be pretty scary, but sharing the experience with other artists is a joy. You have the comfort of asking others to help you, but you also have the excitement of exploring new realms together and the ultimate experience of learning to constructively critique one another's work.

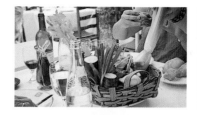

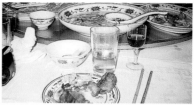

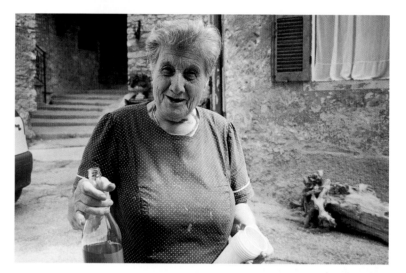

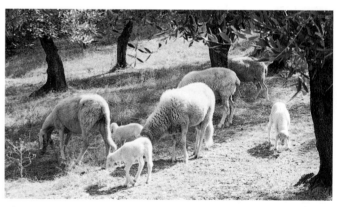

These sheep graze in an olive grove in our backyard.

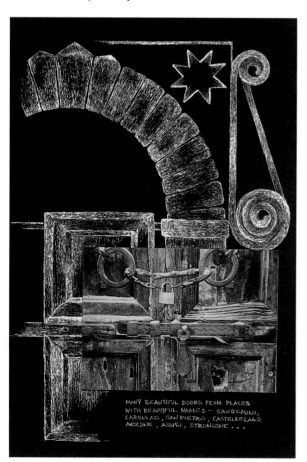

This is a drawing from Marsha Van Buskirk's journal. She documents her travels by integrating her writings and visual interpretations into a journal of her remembrances, 1999.

This visual feast will give you some idea of the variety of work done by artists visiting these little hill towns. All the artists have their own exciting, personal interpretations of the same subject matter.

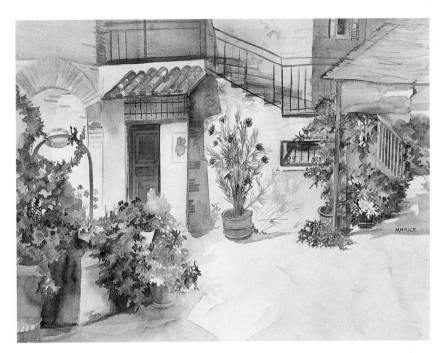

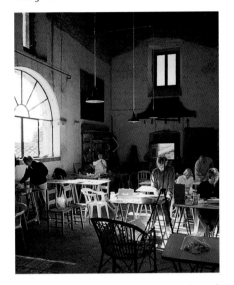

Our studio at LaRomita is the chapel used by the monks dating back to 1548. We are privileged to live and work in an authentic 16th-century monastery.

The grounds at LaRomita provide endless subject matter—the sheep, an English garden, the olive grove, the well, flowers—but one of the favorite subjects is the courtyard. This painting by Mary Rice shows her emotional response to her surroundings, 1999.

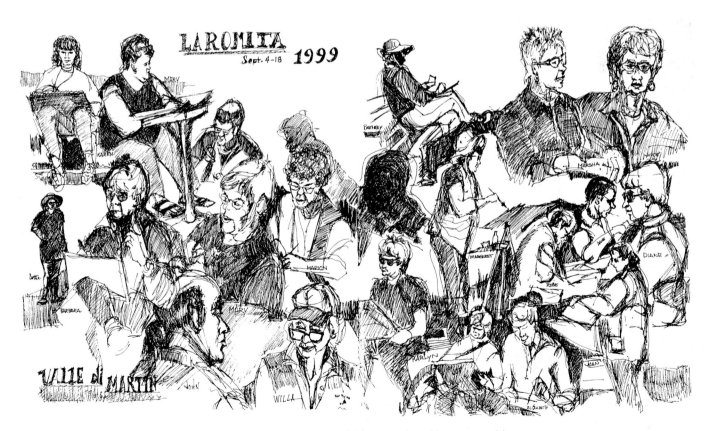

This montage of all the participants on our trip was an ambitious undertaking created by Dottie Burton. She is a master at painting people and capturing their gestures and expressions.

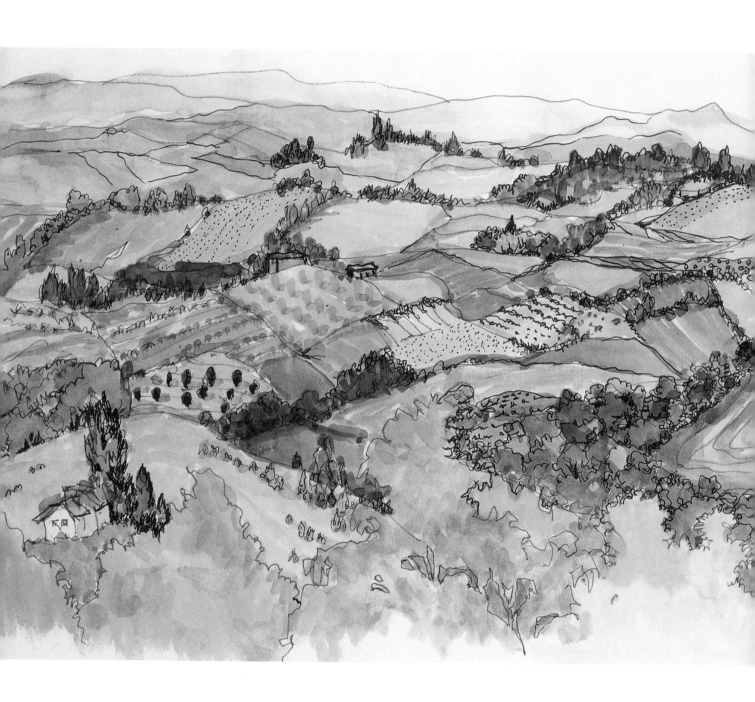

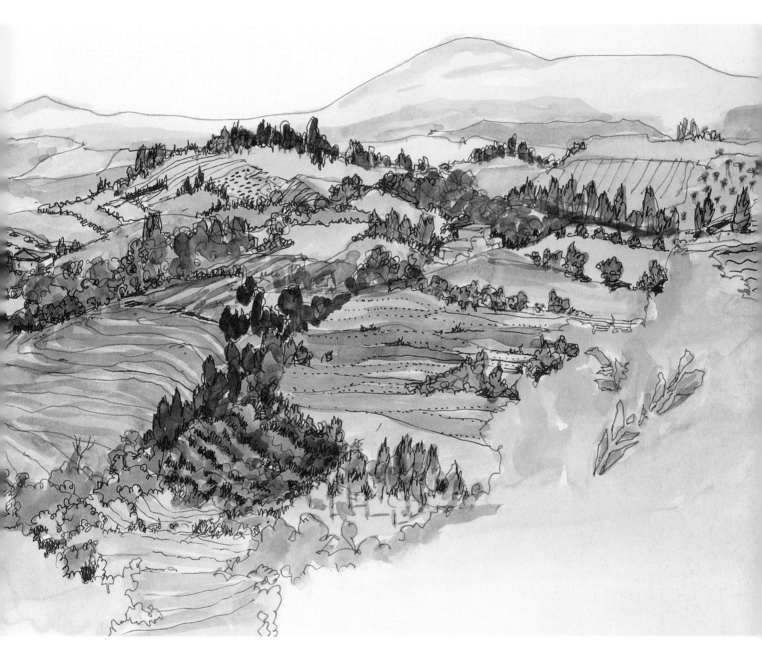

Betty Lynch painted this panoramic view from the
Umbrian hill town of San Gimignano, Italy. Betty
has published a book with sketches and paintings
drawn from her travels. Her watercolors co-exist
with her drawings as equal partners in her art.

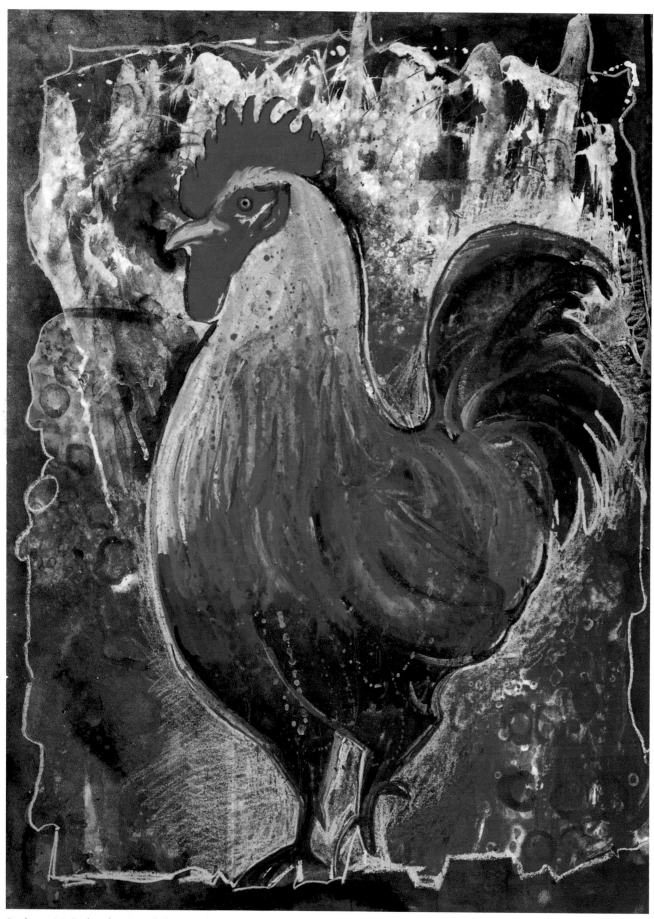

Barbara McFarland painted this cocky rooster in a mixed media format,
using an aura of both cool and hot colors.

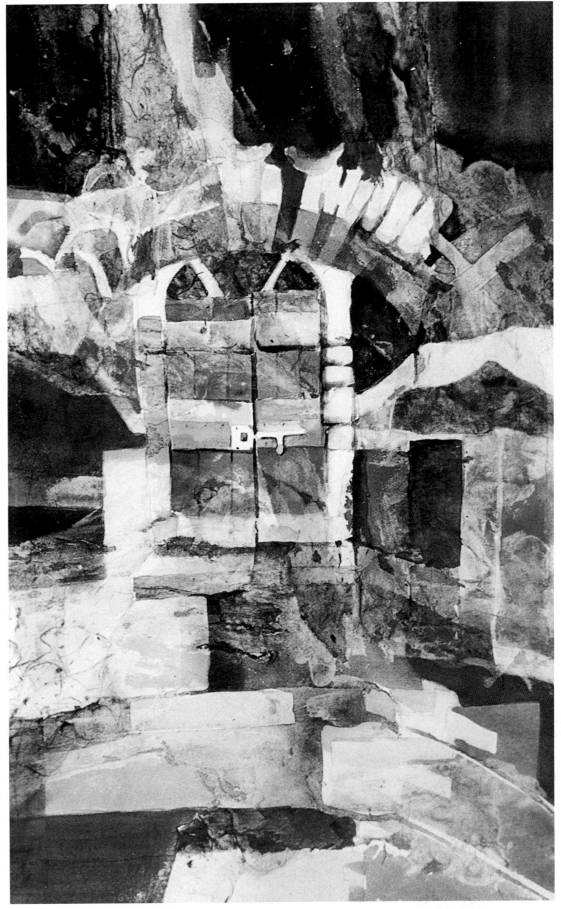

Karen Knutson chose an abstract approach to her subjects. Abstraction requires good design skills and the ability to research and distill the subject to its very essence, 1999.

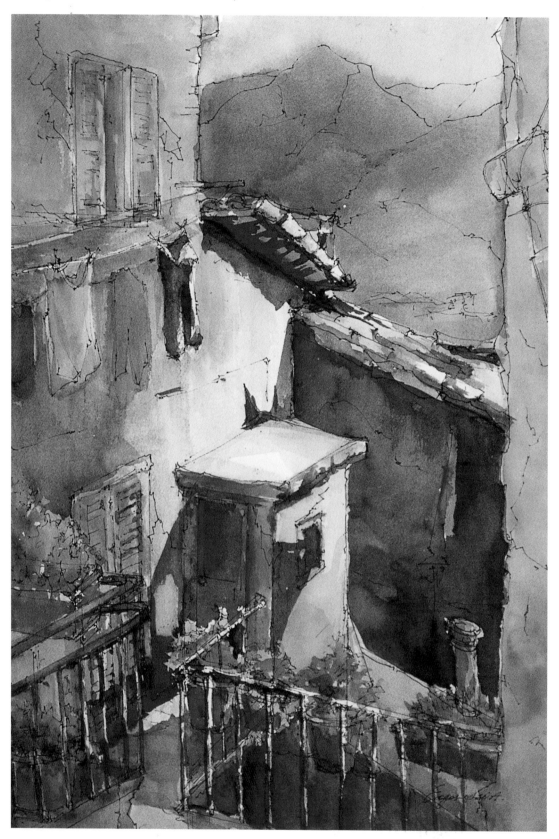

Rose Eager has a flair for using strong contrast and rich color in her work. She works almost exclusively on 300# hot press paper which makes her colors appear more brilliant than if they were used on cold press paper. Her unusual choice of perspective often adds a unique quality to her work.

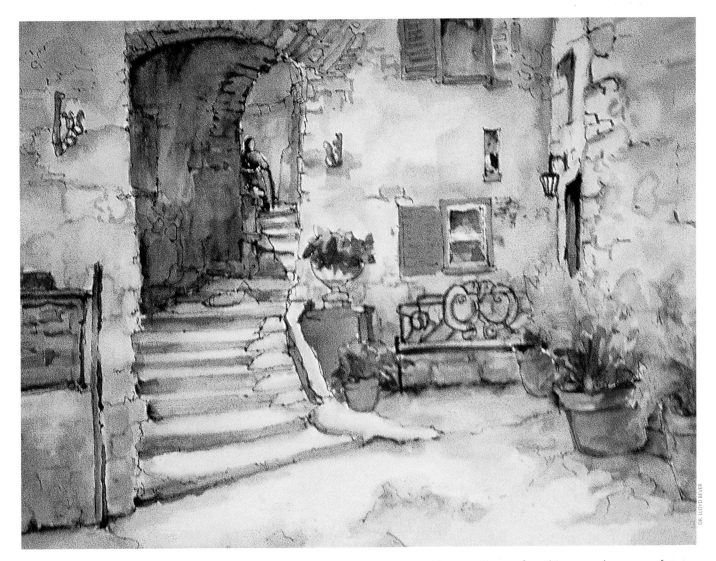

DR. LLOYD BEVER

Margaret Bever painted Valle Di San Martino on 140# Winsor Newton cold press. She prefers this paper because of the smoothness and the lifting potential. Margaret is a master at using luminous darks and adding mystery to her work. In this painting, the darks surround the lights and lead the viewer into the center of interest.

Conclusion. I have had extraordinary experiences combining traveling and painting. Many of these experiences have been funny, such as the day in Ireland when we were perched on the top of a high wharf and a gusty wind took one of the student's palettes and whipped it into the water. The palette landed paint side up and floated around for several hours. Luckily, just prior to our departure, a local fisherman fished it out for us. Another time,

in Umbria, a herd of sheep came over the hill and was headed right for us. We hardly had time to jump up and run when they turned abruptly and headed another direction. When you choose to paint on location, you become entertainment for passersby, you are at the mercy of the weather and the tides, and you never have enough time. In short, life on location is never boring.

Capturing the light...approaches to on-location painting

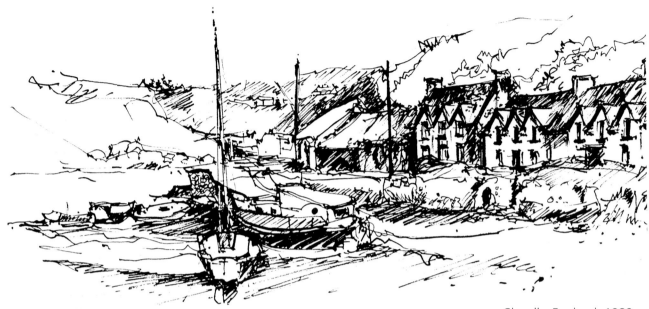

Clovelly, England, 1989.

Begin with a drawing. The more planning you do at this stage, the more freedom you will have when you actually begin painting the subject. Even if your drawings never turn into paintings, they are invaluable because they bring back all the memories of the places you visited. Simply add the date and place next to your name, and you will create a memory that is better than a photograph.

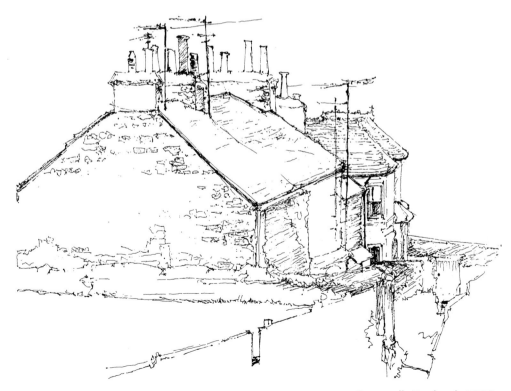

Cornwall, England, 1989.

My personal approach on location is to begin drawing with a pencil or a pen directly on my paper. If I work out a detailed preliminary sketch and then have to redraw it on my final paper, I lose momentum. Once I am satisfied with my drawing, I get out my colors and go for it.

Capturing the light by painting the cool colors first and the warm colors later is probably the most exciting on-location approach because when you paint on location, the light is constantly changing and you have to capture it in a very short time. Early morning and afternoon light are usually very dramatic. Overhead light at noon is flat, while early evening light can by mysterious. Light also reflects off buildings and water and can bounce all over your subject. You can even invent light, placing it wherever your painting needs it and weaving it into your design.

Sometimes, adding only blues and magentas to a sketch completes the painting. Often, the spontaneity of a painting can be lost when it is completed later in a studio using photographs. I prefer to leave the painting at a somewhat unfinished stage, rather than risk losing the essence of the moment.

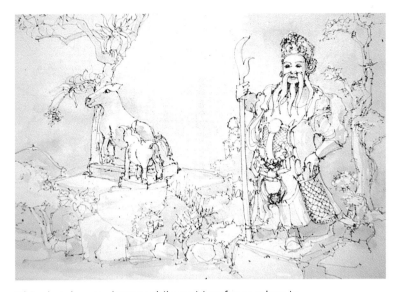

This sketch was drawn while waiting for our bus in Thailand, 1996. The statuary was so inviting and the short space of time so limiting, that I challenged myself to see if I could finish this sketch in fifteen minutes.

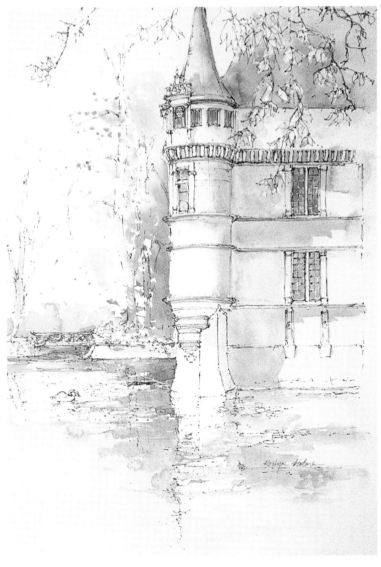

This chateau in France, 1995, posed the same dilemma—a great subject with beautiful reflections and so little time. When it actually came time to finish the painting by adding the warm colors, I decided to stay with the fresh interpretation, rather than risk losing the spontaneity. Sometimes we do our best work when we have limitations pressed upon us.

Cools first and warms later

To begin, start with a puddle of cobalt blue and a puddle of permanent magenta and paint only the cast shadows. Cobalt is a clear, rich color with no violet cast. Keep the paper white in all the areas touched by light. Blues and violets are the complements to the yellows, oranges and reds that will be layered on later. If the shadows fall on an orange-toned surface (stones, fields, etc.), use cobalt blue. If the shadows fall on a yellow-toned surface (buildings, windows, etc.), use the magenta. Sometimes you need to pull a little violet into the blue and sometimes you need to pull a little blue into the violet. When the warm colors are layered on, the colors on the paper will become neutralized or grayed. I am not sure which step is more fun, capturing the light or layering on the warms and watching the lights turn on. By layering pure color, an artist can create a painting that glows with vitality.

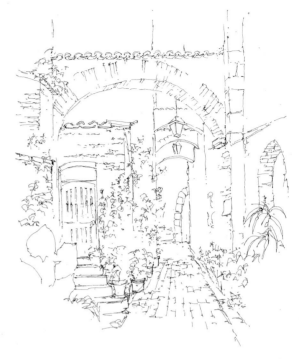

When sketching, try to capture the essence of the subject rather than drawing every stone and leaf. Look for interesting patterns and select only enough information to tell the story.

There are two effective approaches for layering the colors:

• You can charge in the complement while the cool color is still wet, or

• You can let the cool underpainting dry and layer the warm color later.

This demonstration was painted on 140# cold press paper because when the color dries and bonds with the paper, it does not reactivate with the next layer. When designing the patterns of shadows, look for large connecting shapes. These patterns add strength and organization to your painting.

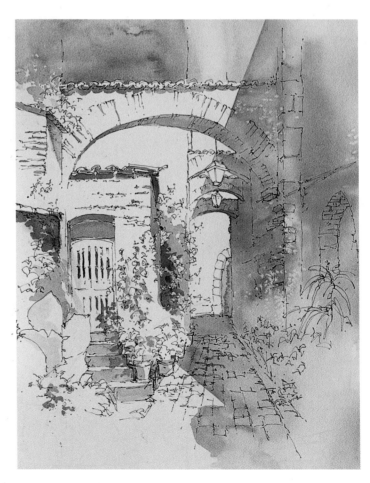

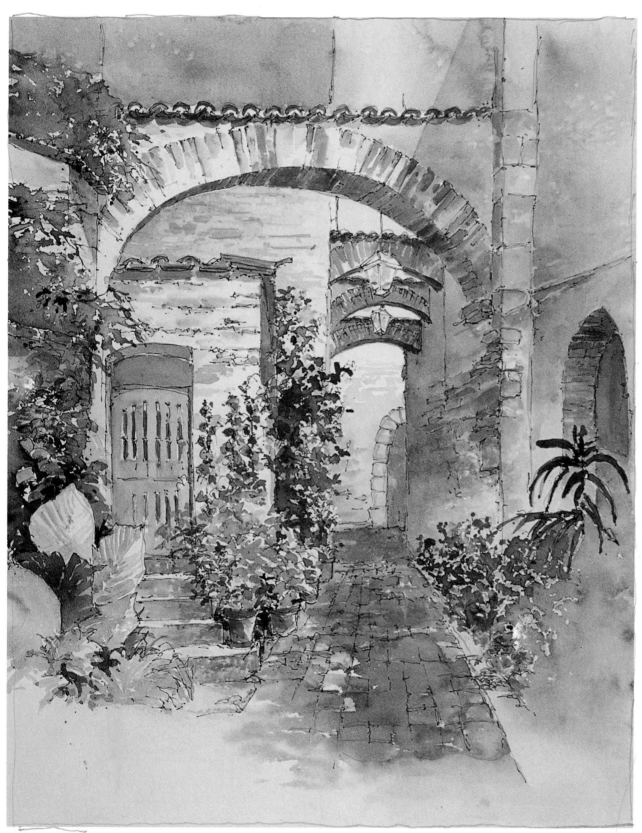

After the cool underpainting is complete, you can begin to add warm colors. To enrich the surface, work in warm, analogous hues. For example, when adding orange, also add yellow and red to achieve harmonic depth. As a finale, consider adding some darks or some areas of bright, pure color.

This painting is called ARCHES ON ARCHES, 1999. The setting is an Umbrian hill town.

Warms first and cools later

The main reason to start a painting with the cools is to capture the light. On days when the light is flat or cloudy, you may choose to start with the warm colors. Or you may find yourself painting a predominantly warm-toned subject, such as the ochre and orange buildings in Italy. For whatever reason, you can reverse this layered approach by starting with warm colors and adding the cast shadows over the top.

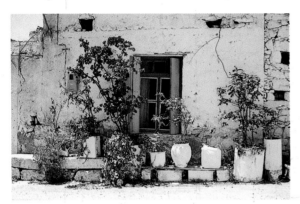 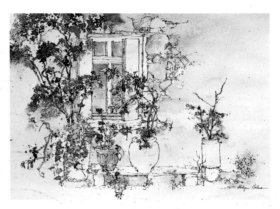

We arrived at our painting site close to noon when the overhead light flattened out the subject. It was also a cloudy day with only a few opportunities to see the cast shadows. I started the painting with foliage, the brick wall and the dark window area.

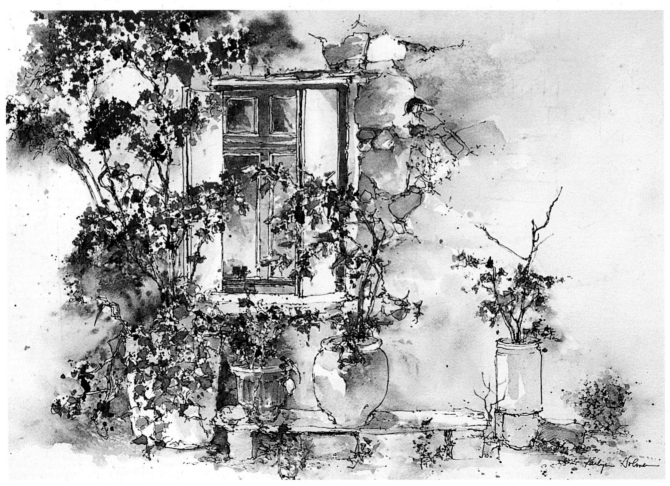

When the sun made one of its rare appearances, I snapped a quick photograph of the cast shadows. When I returned home, I finished the painting in my studio.

Creating a "focus of light"

Staring at white paper can be intimidating. If you prepare a paper with a "focus of light" before you begin to paint, you will create a glow of color that will shine through the finished painting. This formulized underpainting works with any subject. A suggestion you may want to consider is to have a selection of paper surfaces with you when you go on location to paint. I usually bring 140# and 300# cold press paper, 300# hot press paper and a paper with a prepared focus of light. After I have arrived at a location, I select the paper best suited for my subject and begin.

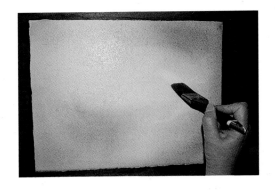

To create this glowing underpainting, saturate both sides of the paper with water. Select a triad of primary colors and apply the colors, using warm near the center of the paper and changing to cool near the edges. Try to leave some white paper near the center. In this

demonstration, I used aureolin yellow, permanent rose and cobalt blue with a little salt for texture. The sketch was drawn on top of the dry underpainting. I did very little painting to finish this piece, adding only a few shadows to pop out the doorways.

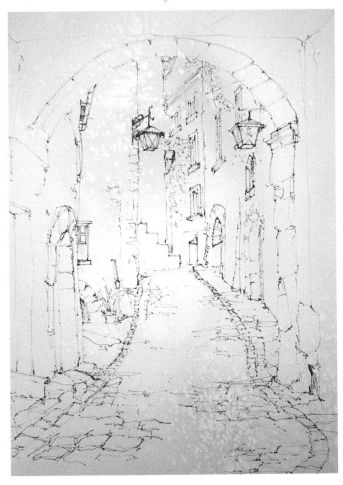

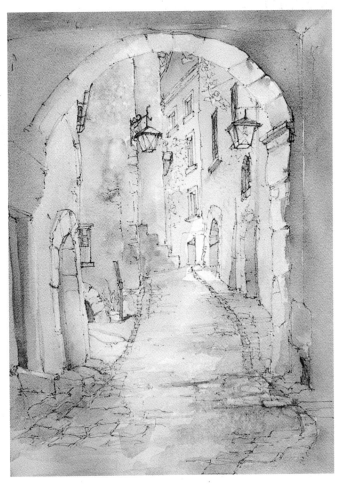

Multiple originals

This is an idea to increase your production and possibly your income, but, best of all, it will increase your ability to paint a subject with various approaches. Why not try all these approaches using only one drawing. Any size pen drawing will work. Simply format it to fit a quarter sheet, or 11" by 15" size. Place your drawing in the photocopier and use 80# Strathmore Aquarius 11 paper.

The heat-set toner is permanent, and this approach provides an opportunity to paint the same image in many different ways. The only paper that works is Strathmore Aquarius 11 because on other papers the toner does not set up. I keep a file of 11" by 15" drawings and reproduce them on demand for demonstrations for Cub Scouts, schools and other volunteer projects.

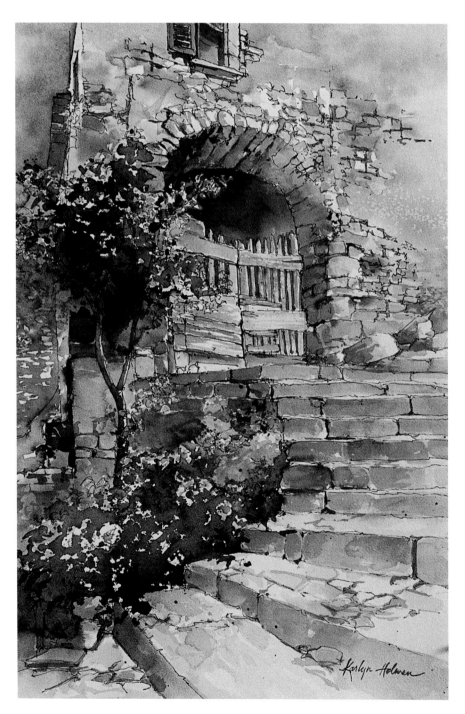

This painting of a typical medieval village in Umbria was completed in two stages, the magenta and cobalt underpainting and the warm layering later. Try to link the lines of design so the viewer's eye can flow from one area to another without getting bogged down with too much detail. Notice how the lines defining the stones link with the doorway and connect with the arch. Toward the edges of the paper, I stopped drawing with the pen and used only paint to suggest some stonework, varying the color between warm and cool.

Suggested approaches:

1. Cools first, warms later.

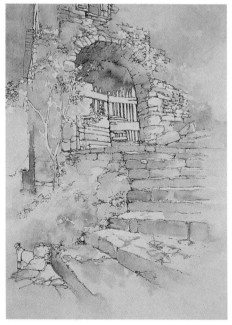

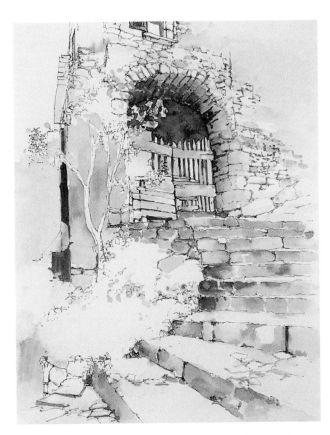

2. Warms first underpainting. To finish, simply add the cast shadows and foliage.

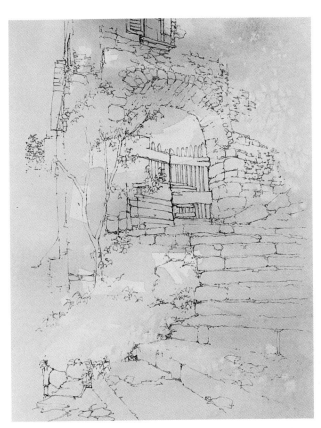

3. Random underpainting. Randomly wet the paper, leaving some areas dry, and then randomly paint the surface.

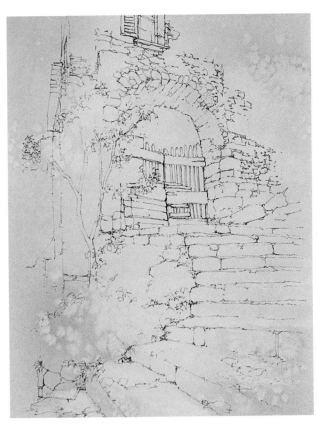

4. Focus of light underpainting. This is probably the most effective way to add a glow to your finished painting.

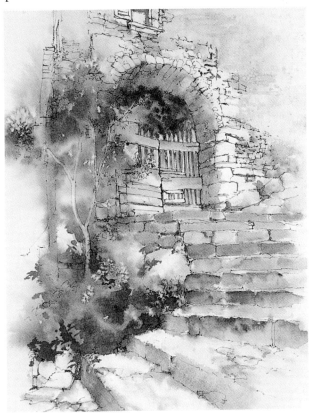

5. Wet-into-wet underpainting. A few crisp edges should move this painting towards completion.

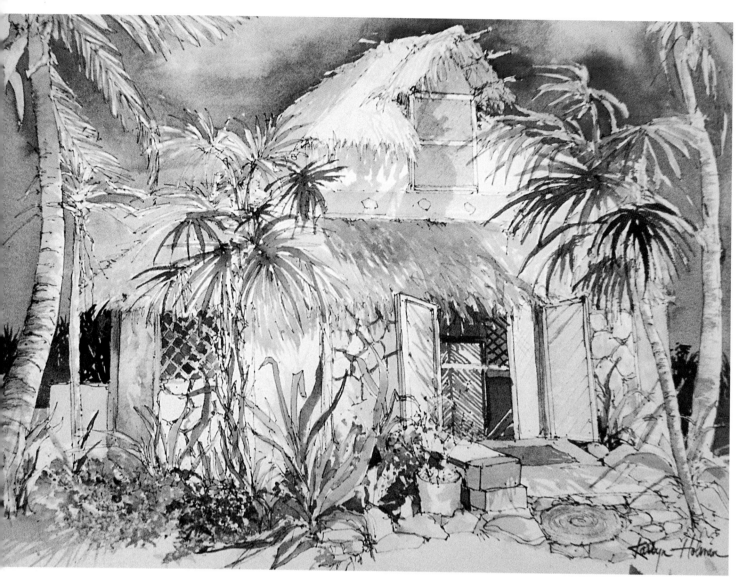

The Caribbean landscape offers brilliant color and exciting textures. This is a painting of our studio at "Punta Pelicano" in the Yucatan. After painting the cast shadows on the front of the studio, I was surprised to see that I had inadvertently created the dancing Mayan figure with a headdress. The fronds of the palm trees were painted light against the dark sky and dark against the light building. Always look for opportunities to transpose values and create contrast.

The transparency of watercolor and the directness of the pen are compatible companions, providing a quick way to interpret travel subjects.

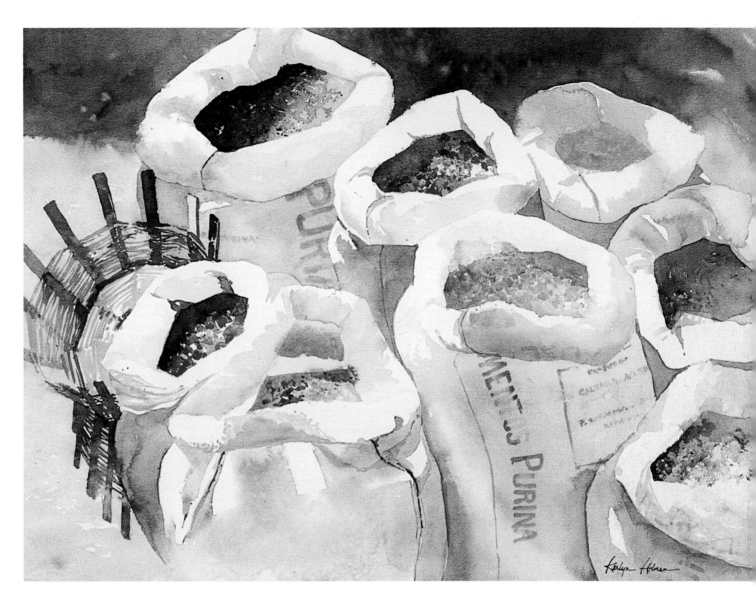

This was a studio painting inspired by photos taken at a market in Guatemala, 1996. All the neutralized grays were achieved by mixing pure complements on the paper. A market scene is a challenging subject to paint on location. These colorful centers of human activity provide a wealth of subject matter. I usually just photograph the scenes for future reference.

Contrasting spontaneity with control...wet-into-wet underpainting

This approach requires many layers of washes and colors, so 140# cold pressed Arches is a good choice of paper because it does not lift the under color with each successive wash. Use masking to achieve the reflected light shapes and the sparkles in the water. Wet both sides of the paper, and using a triad of primary colors, work from warms in the center of your paper to cools close to the edges. I used aureolin yellow, permanent rose and cobalt blue. This triad produces a blended range of colors that encircles the color wheel. Be sure to keep your lightest lights in your interest area. This underpainting creates a glow that will enhance the finished painting.

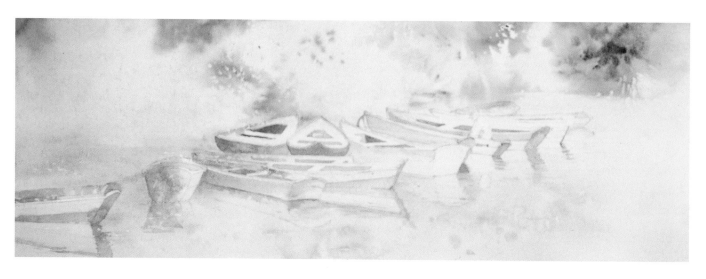

Next, use the puddle method with cobalt blue and permanent magenta to quickly identify the cast shadows. This stage should be painted on dry paper to maintain crisp edges and mid-tone values.

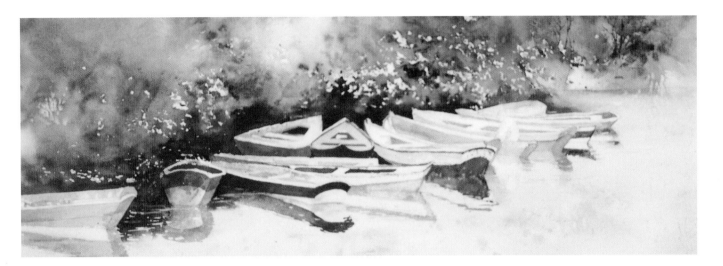

The foliage is created by dropping a pattern of water onto the dry paper using an oriental brush and then flicking yellows, blues and oranges into these drops. While the foliage is still wet, flick in some brown madder and antwerp blue to form the darks along the top edges of the boats. Notice that this dark area is pulled down between the boats and into the water on the right side. Remember to keep the foliage and water subtle, as they serve as a backdrop for the boats. Next, add the reds, yellows and oranges on the boats and in the reflections.

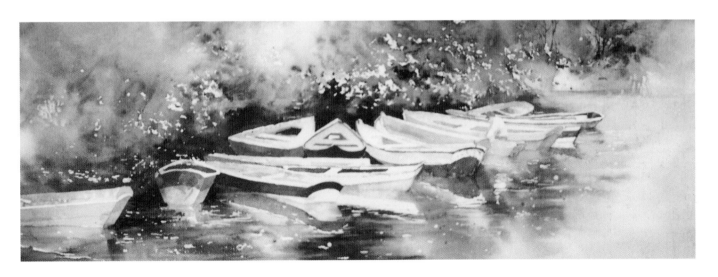

The water is painted wet-into-wet. Carefully wet the entire water area up to the boat line. The foliage colors in the water are Winsor yellow, antwerp blue and quinacridone burnt orange. Allow them to mix together on the wet surface. Only a few mixed greens and darks are added just before the paint dries.

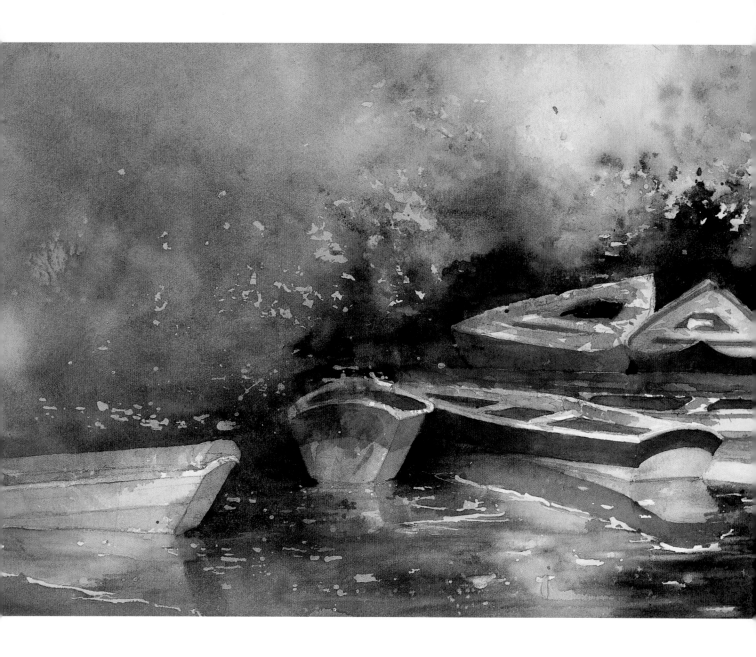

The final step is to add more cast shadows on the boats using cobalt blue and permanent magenta. These flat-bottom boats were in the Marais Poitevin area in France, an extraordinary region nicknamed "Green Venice" because of the hundreds of canals.

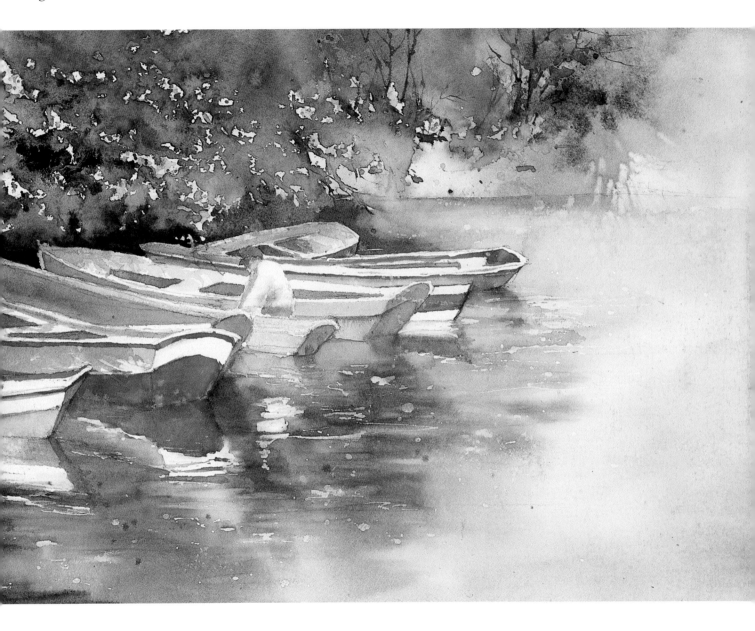

Venice in the rain, 1999.

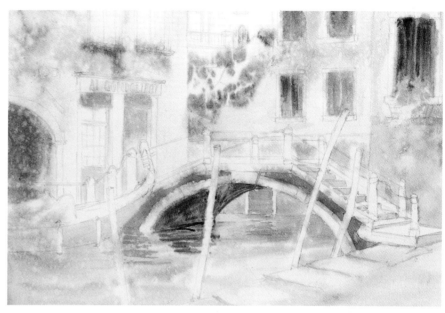

This painting was painted during a steady downpour. I was fortunate to have found a little protected area where I had a great view and was out of the direct rain. To keep the mood of the day, I painted this first wash entirely wet-into-wet. All the edges were soft and moving.

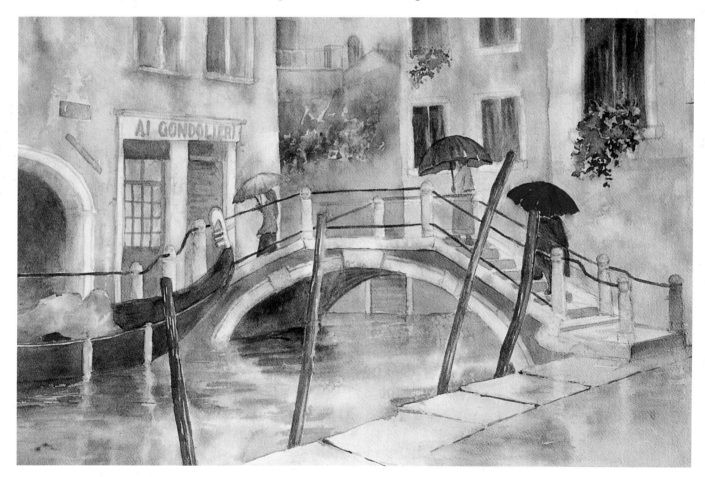

Later, in the studio, I finished the painting using photographs. I decided to add the figures with umbrellas to add more interest to the scene. For the most part, I continued to work wet-into-wet and tried to keep the atmospheric feeling.

Adding figures...creating the center of interest

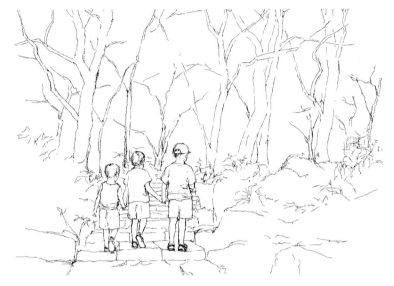

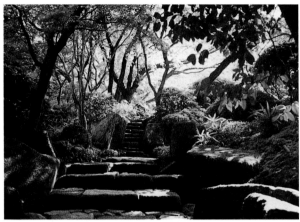

This demonstration will illustrate how you can draw figures into a background. The scale of the figures will dictate whether they will be the center of interest of the painting or merely an interesting element.

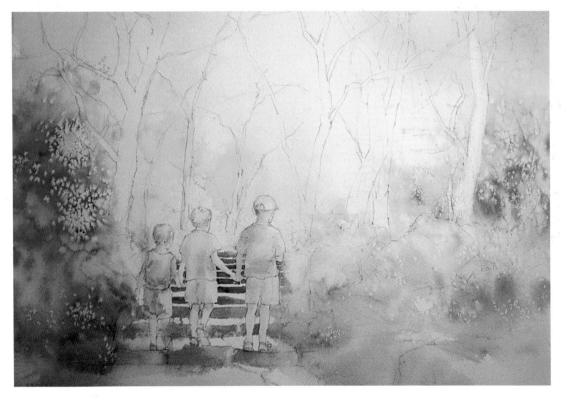

This back-lit painting of figures in a deep woods was actually composed from several photographs. I drew the figures, trees and steps with my HB pencil. I then wet both sides of 140# cold pressed Arches paper and painted a circular focus of light starting with the white paper in the center, radiating to Winsor yellow and raw sienna, then quinacridone burnt orange and on the edges, antwerp blue melting into permanent magenta. I tipped and turned the paper until the colors settled into a glow. This is a "formulized," but very effective way to create a focus of light. To achieve this same effect, select your own triad of primary colors, working warm to cool.

On dry paper, drop patterns of water with your oriental brush where you want the foliage. The patterns are created by dropping puddles of water next to areas of dry paper. Choose warm colors for the center of interest and cool colors towards the edges. I flicked pure Winsor yellow, raw sienna, Winsor orange and quinacridone burnt orange in the center area and the antwerp blue and magenta on the edges. Before the foliage dries, mist the edges of the paper with a fine mister to melt the colors. Leave the center foliage hard-edged.

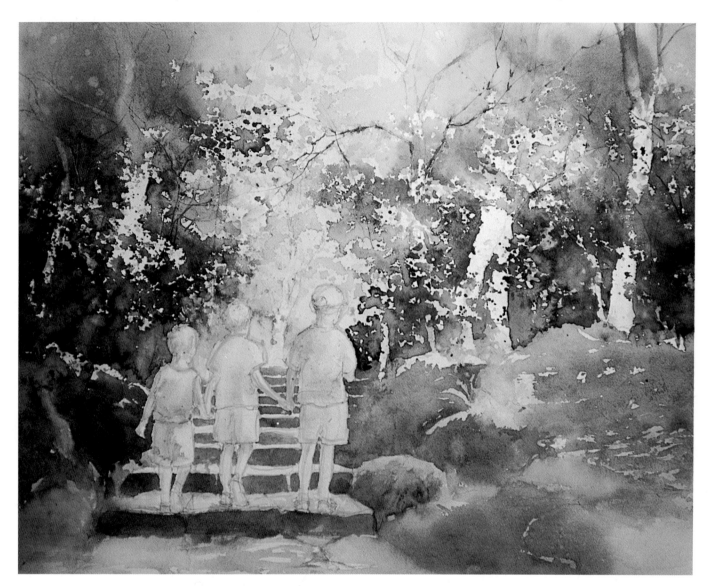

When the paper dries, use the puddle method with cobalt blue and permanent magenta to capture the cast shadows on the steps and on the figures. In an actual back-lit situation, the figures would be entirely in shadow. I chose to use more light on the boys so they would become the center of interest.

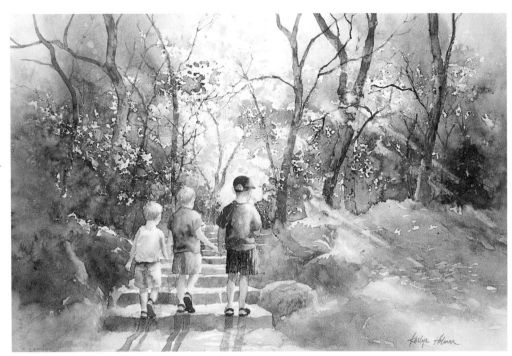

The tree trunks can be added after the foliage dries. The branches are painted with a small #4 painting knife with a rounded tip. This technique is used in oil painting, but works well with watercolor. Try to achieve contrast between the crisp tree branches and the soft foliage. In my painting, I painted the local (actual) color on the boys' clothing to make them the center of interest. The red hat provides a dark contrast to the light background, and the light heads of the other boys serve as a contrast to the dark background. This technique is called transposition—dark against light and light against dark. The light peeking through the trees was created by lifting the color with a damp tissue or a damp Q-tip®.

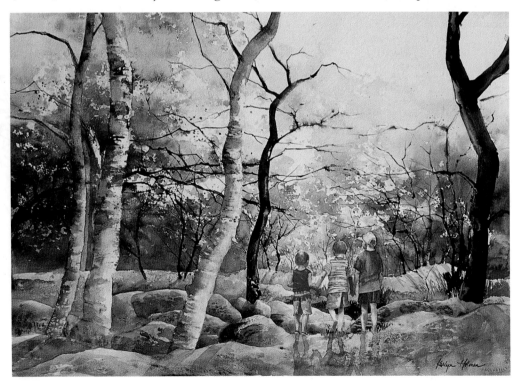

Kerry Woods, 1999.

As the artist, you may decide the scale of the figures. In my demonstration painting, I made the figures larger, creating a more intimate view. In this painting of the Kerry Woods in Ireland, I made the figures smaller, thus switching the center of interest to the light filtering through the trees. The figures add interest, but are not the focal point.

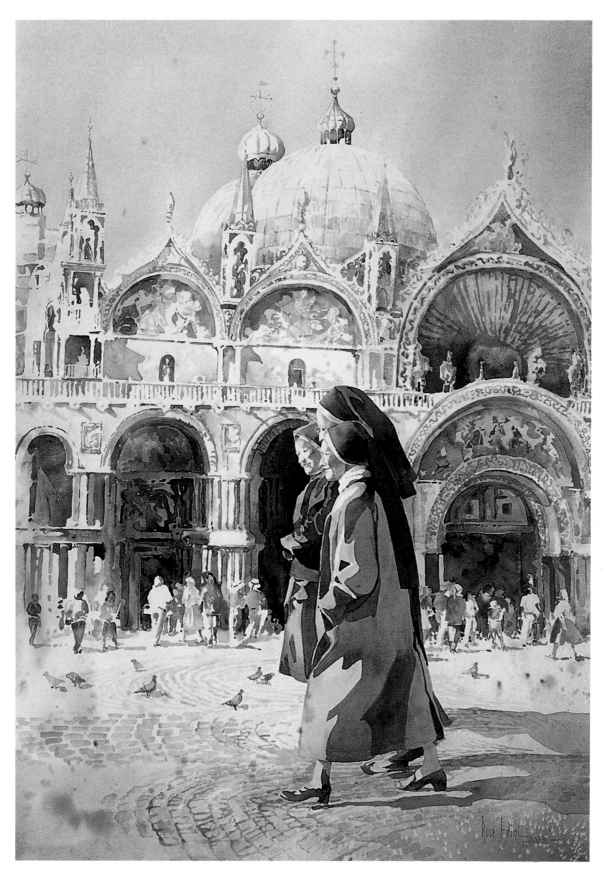

In this beautiful painting by Rose Edin, the scale of the figures varies. The figures in the background are colorful and enrich the painting, but the nuns in the foreground are the focal point and make this painting unique.

St. Mark's Saints, Venice, Italy by Rose Edin. Reprinted from *Watercolor Workshop 2* by Rose Edin, Walter Foster Publishing, Inc., 1992.

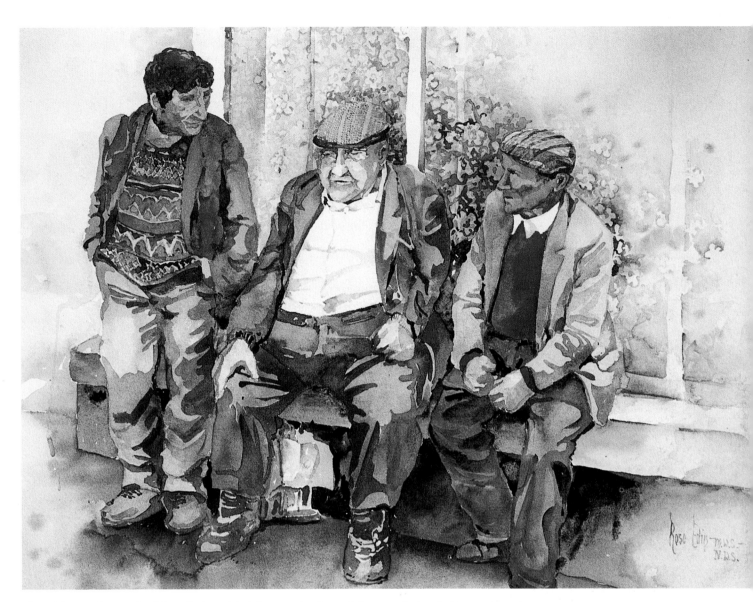

The Irish gentlemen in this painting titled BLARNEY by Rose Edin are obviously the center of interest in this delightful composition. The background suggests linear space divisions, as well as lacy curtains, but the focus of the painting is on the wonderful expressions and gestures of the men.

Designing space...multiple images

This type of abstraction entails designing space so that the separate elements of the painting have an opportunity to explore the motif in depth. Dig in and really get to know and feel the subject until you have exhausted the possibilities. Another way to express this interest is to show multiple interpretations of a similar subject. Pick subject matter with a coherent theme. Subjects such as seasons, rocks, reflections or water are possible choices. The challenge is to paint with directional movement that flows within believable boundaries so the piece does not look patched together.

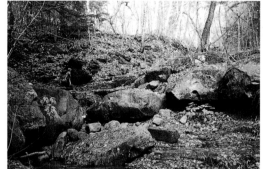

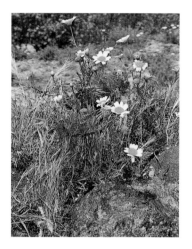

Rocks and flowers are two of my favorite subjects. In the painting below, I placed the emphasis on the water and rocks and freely drew the flowers from one shape to another as a means of tying the shapes together.

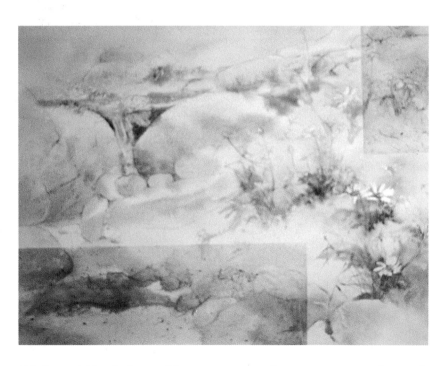

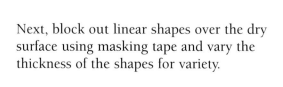

Work on 140# Arches cold press paper and glue several pieces of cut oriental paper for added shape, color and texture. Draw your image, allowing the lines to cross over the various paper surfaces. Mask any areas where you may want to save the pure whites. I masked a few daisies and the directional lines of movement in the water. Wet the entire piece and apply the colors wet-into-

wet. To achieve the soft out-of-focus foliage, the calligraphy was added while the surface was still wet. No tape was used in the underpainting.

Next, block out linear shapes over the dry surface using masking tape and vary the thickness of the shapes for variety.

The following compositional guidelines will help you achieve a sense of unity in your design:

Look for **connecting lines of movement**.

Choose **varying size relationships**, such as long rectangles, squares, organic shapes, etc.

Balance shapes, such as positive next to negative, realistic next to abstract, etc.

Work on **transitional areas** so they connect naturally.

Think about **contrast**. Design smooth surfaces next to textured surfaces, busy places next to quiet places, darks next to lights, cools next to warm, soft next to crisp.

Use **lost and found edges**. Allow some edges to disappear and lead the eye to the adjoining area by using similar values next to each other or by leaving a rest area.

The **connecting linear shapes** are designed to provide directional movement and rhythmic patterns that entertain as well as guide the viewer from one shape to another.

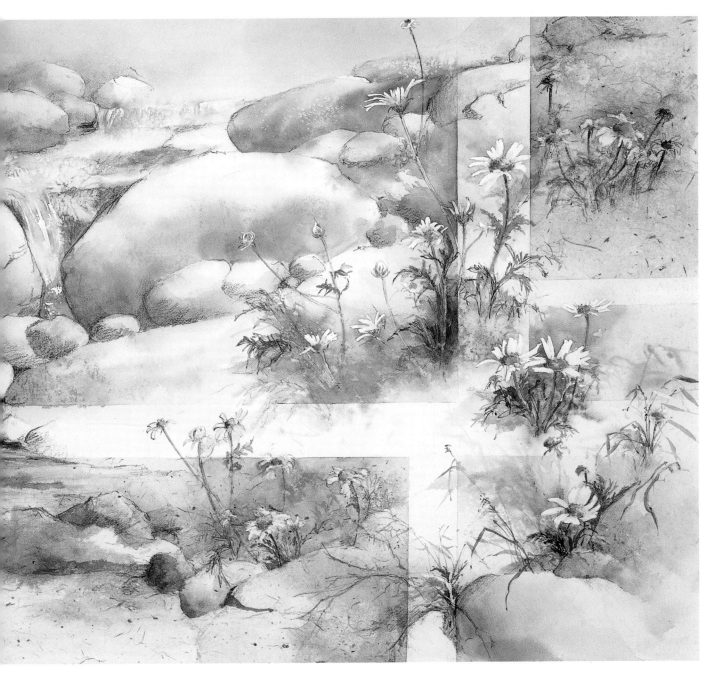

Designing space using a theme

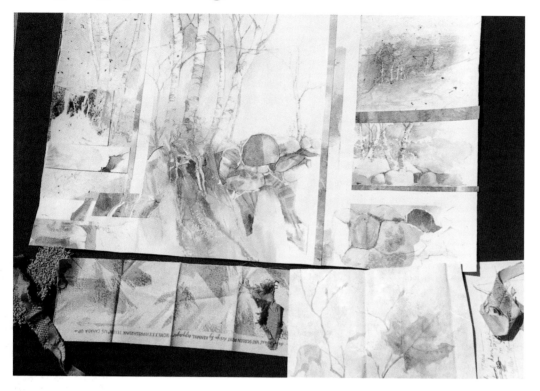

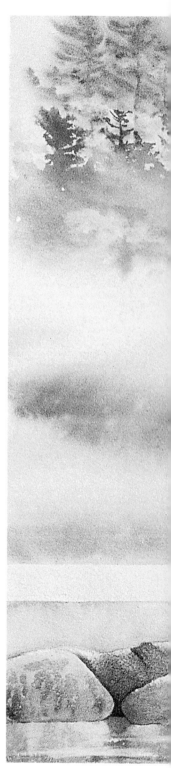

The theme of this painting was to meet someone else's expectations and match their existing color scheme. Accepting commissions often helps you grow as an artist because you generally have to paint subjects you would not have chosen. As it turned out, I really enjoyed this commission.

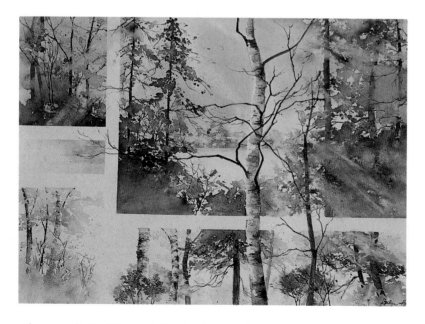

The woods in fall are full of colors and patterns and have always provided me with endless inspiration.

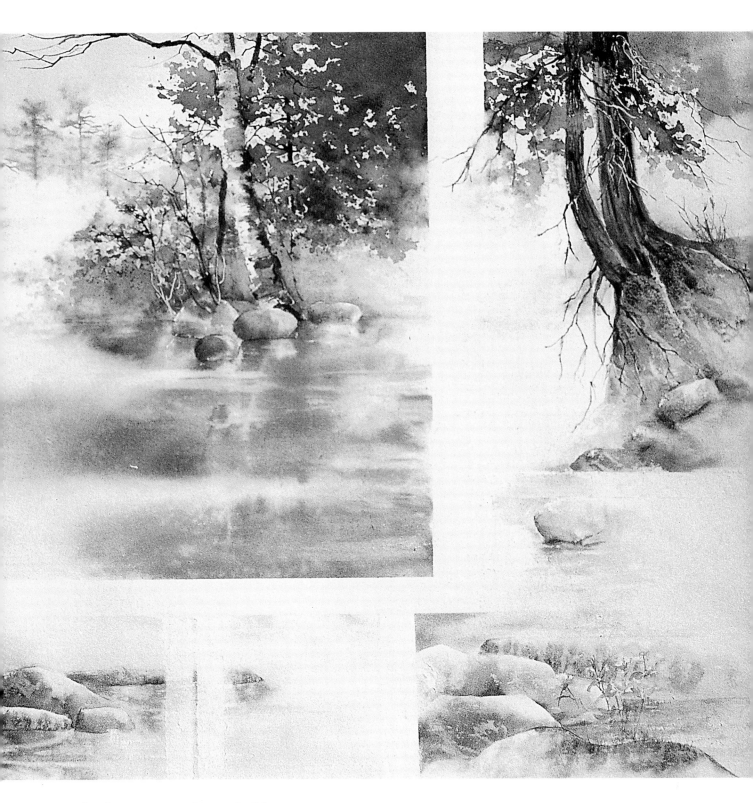

Water and reflections provide wonderful contrasts for lost and found edges. This subject also allows close in-focus detail and panoramic vistas simultaneously, offering the best of both perspectives.

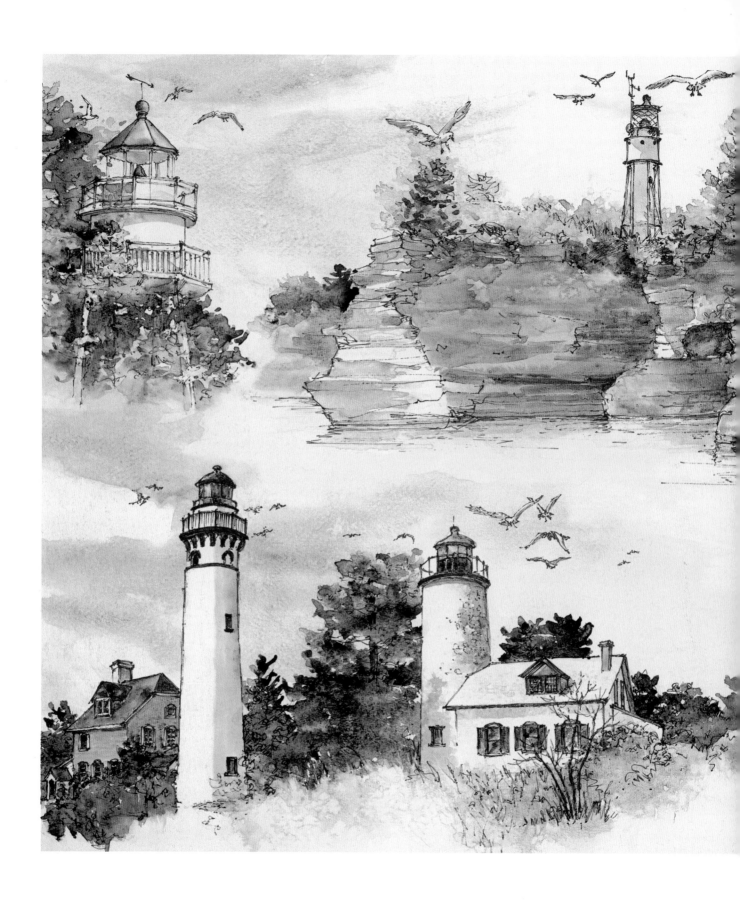

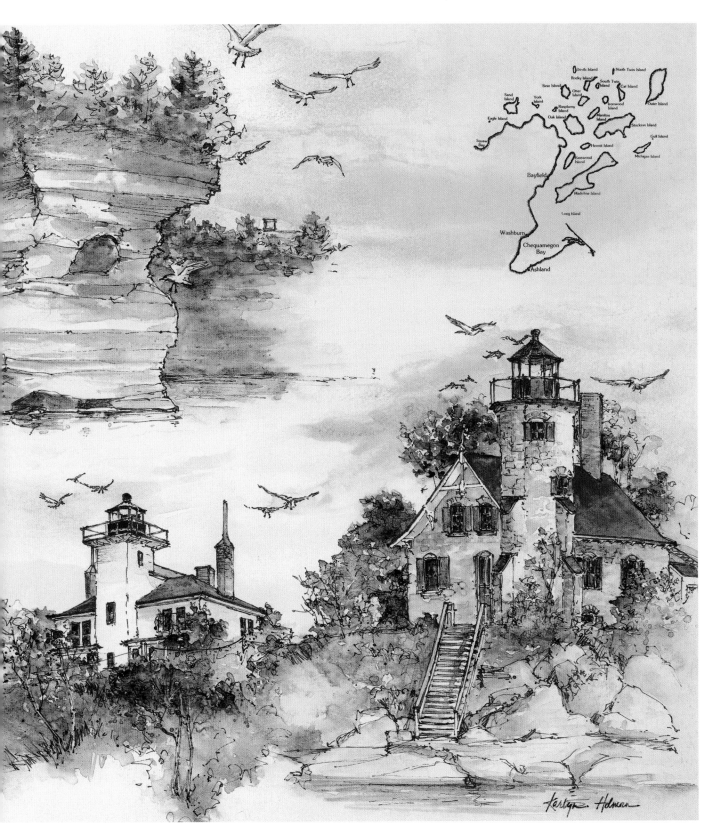

Lighthouses of the Apostle Islands, Lake Superior.
This painting was a challenge because each lighthouse
varied in scale. I decided to feature the Rocky Island
lighthouse (top center) and group the others on a
descending land formation. I added the birds as
a unifying design element.

Using fibered paper as an underpainting...creating transitions

This lesson provides a somewhat abstract, alternative way to understructure your paintings. This under layer affects the end result and provides a textured surface. One of the most difficult aspects of painting is developing an awareness of how to create effective transitions from one area to another in your work. For example, painting hard edges next to hard edges is not as effective as painting hard edges next to a series of subtle or lost edges. Fibered papers provide varied transitions that give unexpected accents. The dynamic planes of texture created by these layered papers add a dimensional, almost magical quality.

To prepare a painting ground, glue down randomly torn pieces of several varieties of oriental paper. Some of the papers are earth tones like the washi paper from Japan, some are white like the Thai fibered unryu, and some have small bark-like pieces like the chiri paper. Allow the papers to dry before you begin your painting.

Simply draw directly over the textured papers and let the fun begin. Keep an open mind as your painting progresses. You may feel slightly "out of control" because you are trying to draw over different textures and dried glue, but you will be surprised with the results.

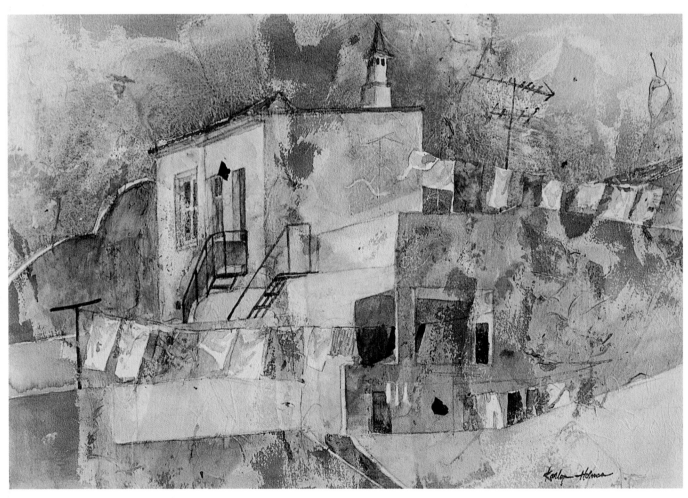

This subject has very subtle value contrast because most of the light was bouncing around the predominantly white-washed stone. The laundry on the lines was mostly white, the steps were white, and I found it challenging to build in any value contrast. By interpreting the scene with randomly applied oriental papers, I created light and dark value changes where I least expected them. Applying the color was so much fun because it floated over the various oriental papers and created exciting textures. Choosing ultramarine blue for the sky added another strong value contrast.

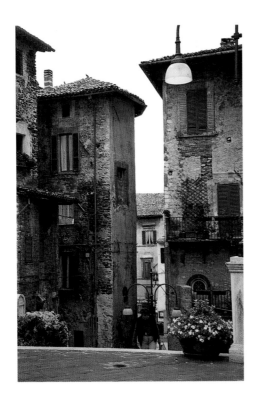

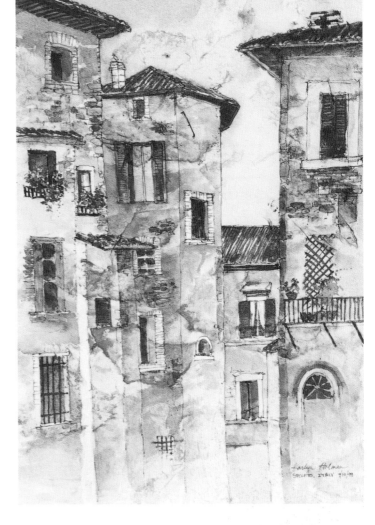

Spoleto, Italy, 1999. Working in the rain under umbrellas, we still found inspiration in these dark medieval buildings. By working on a prepared ground of oriental papers, we unveiled random textures that appeared and disappeared, making this process an exciting adventure.

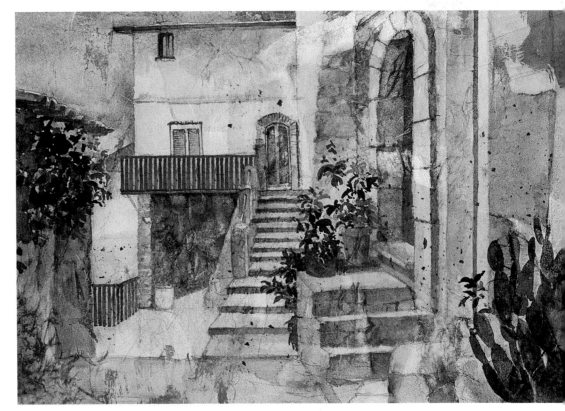

Stronecone, Italy, 1997. The Umbrian hill towns are very quiet. Often the sounds of a baby crying or church bells ringing are the only things that remind you that you are not alone.

Marketing your skills...it can be more fun than you think

I can not pass up this opportunity to share another passion I have, and that is being a businessperson. I joined the real world of business in 1968, when I opened my own studio/gallery. I love meeting the people who come into my gallery. Although operating your own business can be all-consuming, set your priorities so you can stay focused on your creative side. After thirty-two years, I now have six employees who do the book-keeping, framing and day-to-day operations, so I am free to lead this blessed life of travel-ing and painting. I try to have a show every year or so outside my area, but basically I market all my artwork in my own gallery. I can paint a picture one day and frame and hang it on the wall the next day. You have to make choices about how you market your paintings. You may choose to seek gallery representation, have open houses at your home, participate at art fairs, or offer your work via the Internet. Whatever your choice, consider the following suggestions:

Keep good records. This can be done in a simple spiral-bound notebook or a simplified computer program. An accounting of expenses and income is necessary whether you have your own business or have someone else sell your work.

Invest in some **business cards**, **stationary**, and possibly a **brochure**. Consider getting an **e-mail address** and a **website**. My website has generated a few sales, but it has been invaluable for informing students about my workshops and travel adventures. Check out my website at www.karlynholman.com.

Consider producing **multiples** of your best work when you are ready. Cards and small prints give me a low end product, so I can paint almost exclusively in a larger format. If your work is extremely detailed, you only have to paint the work once and get paid for your effort many times. With today's choices in reproduction methods, you can profitably reproduce an image one time or a thousand times.

Take **slides and prints** of each painting to document your work. A portfolio of slides of all your work is absolutely indispensable. This historical and photographic trail of your paintings provides a visual record of your growth and is an excellent way to document your progress. If you decide to enter a show, you will have the slides all ready to go.

Prepare a **resume** documenting your shows, published articles, and other important information.

Design a **certificate of authenticity**. This document makes you appear more profession-al and informs your buyers that you care enough to give them your full address and inform them about their rights. The certificate provides a record of who purchased your paintings, when they purchased them and how much they paid. I put these names in a database and use this list to send mailings and invitations to showings.

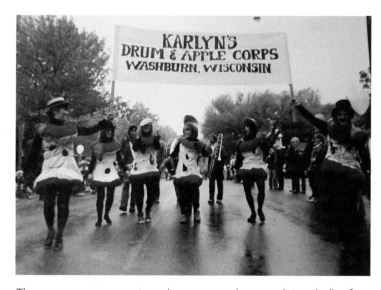

There are many ways to gain exposure (no pun intended)—for over 20 years "Karlyn's Drum & Apple Corps" has marched in the Bayfield Apple Festival parade.

"Lease to own" sales policy

A sales technique that has been extremely successful at my gallery has been my "lease to own" policy. I started this program in 1984 with a little sign posted in my sales gallery that read "Rent a Painting, $10.00 a month." In the first year I rented (and sold) sixty-six paintings through this program. This successful idea broadened my market base and gave me incentive to get busy and paint more paintings. The low monthly, interest-free payment allowed otherwise unqualified buyers like newlyweds, retirees and college students to take home my paintings. The second year I rented (and sold) 136 paintings. This program gives me a year 'round cash flow, which is a huge benefit for me because I have a seasonal business. The very low monthly payment had too slow of a return, so I have since changed the format, but I have no regrets about my early program. Of the thousands of paintings I have sold over the last sixteen years, only three buyers defaulted.

I modified the program by using this simple formula. I take the purchase price and divide it into ten monthly payments. I still do not charge interest and I allow customers to trade in their paintings on another painting. People rarely trade, but knowing they have the option to trade often convinces them to enter the program.

Pros and Cons. The advantages of this type of program far outweigh the disadvantages for the artist and the customer.

• Because of the increased sales, I am very motivated to paint. This lease program has become my outlet for experimental paintings, travel paintings and any subject I want to paint. I do very few commissions.

• I no longer feel obligated to paint in all price ranges. The lessees can buy what they *like* instead of what they *can afford*, and I can paint whatever I want to paint.

• This is the best benefit! The program generates sales to corporations, small businesses and professional offices which often purchase several paintings at one time. I once sold forty-six paintings to one businessperson for use in offices.

• The main disadvantage of this program is that the bookkeeping can be burdensome. However, the monthly communication with the customer can be an advantage. By the time a painting is paid in full, we have sent nine billings. This means we have had nine opportunities to communicate with these customers. I use this opportunity to invite them to shows, introduce a new print or even proclaim the birth of a new grandchild. These customers become friends and come back to buy more artwork.

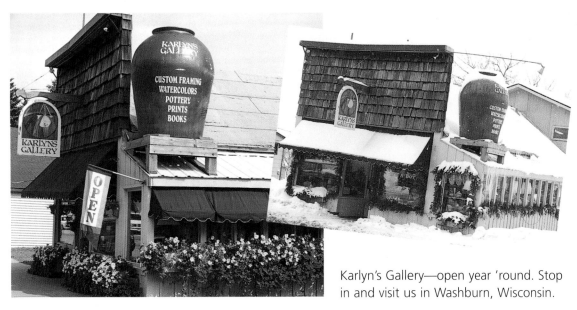

Karlyn's Gallery—open year 'round. Stop in and visit us in Washburn, Wisconsin.

ART RENTAL/PURCHASE AGREEMENT

Karlyn's Gallery
Karlyn Holman
318 West Bayfield St.
Washburn, WI 54891
715-373-2922
karlyn@win.bright.net
www.karlynholman.com

Date _____

The lessee agrees to rent/purchase the work of art for 10% down and 10% per month for the following nine months.

_____ {Lessee}, agrees to lease the work of art listed below on the following terms:

1. The work of art leased or rented is described as follows:
   Title _____
   Dimensions _____
   Value/Purchase Price _____

2. This work of art is an original, created by Karlyn Holman. The artist reserves all copyright rights.

3. Lessee will pay a rental fee of $ _____ per month, payable on the first of each month. Lessee has the option of applying 100% of the rental fee to the purchase with no interest charged. If the Lessee changes his/her mind and decides to purchase another painting, the rental fee will be transferred in full to that painting.

4. Lessee is liable for all loss, theft, damage or deterioration of the work.

5. Lessee agrees the work(s) will not be used for reproduction, unless agreed upon by the artist.

Special arrangements _____
Lessee _____
Address _____
City, State, Zip _____
Phone _____
Buyer _____
Seller _____

Here is a copy of my "lease to own" agreement, which is very simple and easy to understand. I put all the "lessees" in a database and when I have a show, I can easily access all the zip codes in close proximity and invite those customers to the opening. They always bring friends and relatives, and even if they don't buy a painting, their presence makes the opening a gala event.

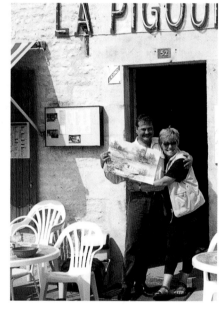

Another reason to paint on location is the opportunity to sell your paintings. This gentleman in France paid me 100 francs more than I suggested and even bought me lunch (he owned the restaurant).

Karlyn Holman Instructional Videos currently available:

Five-day Workshop. This six-hour video was filmed live during a five-day workshop. Subjects taught include abstract painting, portrait painting, wildflowers in a design, and capturing light on water lilies. $15.00

Abstract Expression. Filmed in Karlyn's studio, this four-hour video provides instruction in collage, non-objective painting, as well as abstracting a subject. $20.00

The Landscape in Watercolor. This four-hour video teaches how to capture light and mood, painting in many seasons, and technical aspects of painting a landscape. $20.00

Illustrated Children's Picture Books (all hard cover) by Karlyn:

Christmas Song of the North by Marsha Bonicatto. $14.95
Little Brother Moose by James Kasperson. $16.95
Grandpa's Garden by Shea Darian. $16.95
Ditch of Witches by Warren Nelson. $16.95

To order, please contact:
   Karlyn's Gallery
   318 E. Bayfield St.
   Washburn, WI 54891
   Phone or Fax: 715-373-2922
   E-mail: karlyn@win.bright.net
   Website: karlynholman.com

Conclusion

Staying on the path to your own personal expression

On your journey toward finding your own personal mark, think of yourself as a student—always learning, always searching and eventually growing into your own personal expression. The excitement of new beginnings keeps your mind open to a new vision. As you explore and discover, enjoy every aspect of your work, from conception to the final details. Each step is important. Developing this passion for watercolor takes a lot of courage and commitment and continuing to grow and stay excited is a big challenge. Here are a few tips to help you along the way:

Find a trusted artist companion to share your journey. As artists, we must share, as sharing leads to growth and self-discovery. Trusted artist friends often may provide the most valuable critiques.

Combine travel and painting. Painting on location will expand your observation powers and challenge your drawing skills.

Join an art organization, watch artists demonstrate, ask questions and become part of an artist community. Since I have developed a passion for watercolor, I have discovered a camaraderie unmatched by any other profession.

Always keep at least one of your good paintings as an anchor piece to help you through those difficult transitional times or when you are suffering from artist block.

Keep yourself visually stimulated by visiting galleries, museums and art openings, checking out what is available on the Internet and collecting art books.

Go to your studio and paint, paint, paint. Each painting leads to another painting. Keep the momentum going and keep it *fun and free*.

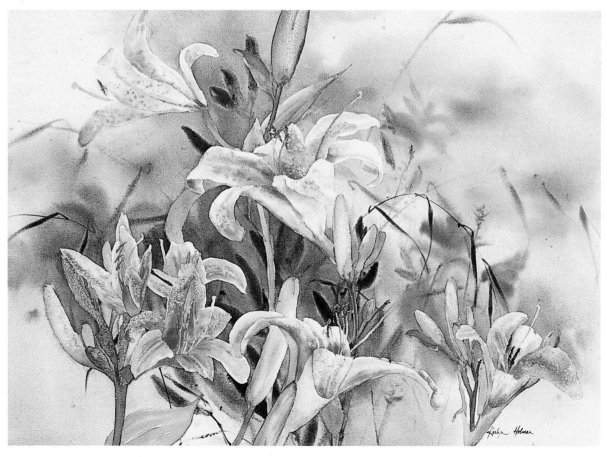

Index